ATTITUDE:
A STUDY IN PHILIPPIANS

JEFF LEIS

Author:
Pastor Jeff Leis

Editing:
Polly Alterman
Sherry Macias
Mark Matsumoto
Toni Sanchez
Matt Shumaker

Design:
Sarah Kohn

Art Direction:
Matt Shumaker

Video Production:
Sarah Kohn
Ian Rough
Matt Shumaker

Published by Yosemite Church
© 2017 Jeff Leis
First printing 2017

Printed in the United States of America

TABLE OF CONTENTS

PREFACE

Learning to cultivate a deep and abiding love for and trust in Jesus requires attention, devotion and perseverance. When we are able to calibrate our lives to an awareness of His presence, we discover an increased ability to make adjustments that keep our attitude synchronized with the Spirit. For me, this journey has been the theme and objective of my life - to stay in sync with the heart of God and the mind of Christ. I have probably failed as much as I have succeeded. Yet God continues his refining work and his peace continues to grow within me.

From my earliest connection to the Scriptures, I have loved the Book of Philippians. It illustrates a profound affection for other believers and a radical surrender to Christ that echoes through Paul's relational instructions. The first can only be sustained as the second is cultivated.

It is this cultivation that I hope and pray will become more intuitive for those who read, study, and meditate on this material and the Scriptures that have inspired it. Until we recognize and take ownership of our mental state and condition, synchronization with the Spirit will elude us.

I have read numerous commentaries on the book of Philippians and have never come across someone who postulated that attitude was its dominate theme. That puts me in check to substantiate why or how I would then propose such a theme. There are two prominent concepts that weave themselves through this little book. The first and most dominant concept is *rejoicing*. Sixteen times the word *joy* or *rejoice* is used, which sounds like attitude to me. Philippians 4:4 says, *"Rejoice in the Lord always. I will say it again: rejoice!"*

The second prominent word used 11 times, is the Greek word *Phroneo* which means to set one's mind or heart upon something; to have understanding and to be wise. It is more than intellectual activity; it includes emotional connection as well. It often describes a pattern of thought and direction of the heart. This combination of concepts and words are what produce one's attitude. It is impossible to even approach a spirit that rejoices always without an increased mindfulness of Christ's presence and his promise to accomplish his purposes within us (Philippians 1:6 and 2:12-13).

The more one's life becomes dependent upon Christ and his perspective, the more intuitive we become at spiritually regulating our attitude and disposition. As we discover greater and greater access to His power within us, we also discover a greater ability to display His kindness and love. When this becomes the new normal for the believer, their influence and impact are not just increased but also magnified. This augmented mindfulness produces a joyfulness that reflects Christ's purposes and an attitude that reflects his presence (Philippians 4:5).

One of the most strategic commitments we can make to cultivate our attitude is to foster conversations that invite Christ's perspective. I can remember being a child waking up with a grumpy attitude and coming up the stairs of our old farmhouse in eastern Colorado. I would enter into the kitchen, where my mother was usually cooking, and be either sulking or unresponsive. She would say to me, "Jeffrey Paul, you got up on the wrong side of your bed. Go back to your room and get up on the right side of your bed." The message was clear. I had the power to choose what kind of attitude and disposition I was going to bring into that day. On my own I was struggling to alter my attitude, but with a little help from my dear mother I was reminded that I could choose how I would enter that day.

This is true for all of us as children of God. The Spirit of Christ is always present, wanting to remind us that there is another side to our bed; another perspective that we can choose. As a child I didn't have the insight of God's perspective or the awareness of his promises and presence. Becoming a growing disciple within a Christian community is one of the ways we cultivate conversations that enable us to alter our attitudes when they falter. The process of becoming more like Christ always flows through a conversation. This conversation is ultimately with God, but is equally going on within ourselves and can be stimulated and improved through dialogue with others. Someone once said, "thoughts disentangle themselves as they pass through our lips and our fingertips."

My hope is that you, the reader, will engage in many rich and revealing conversations. That you will discover the conversations that are going on inside of you - the old, tainted and often deceptive voices that lure you away from the voice of the Spirit of truth. And finally, that you will write, journal and learn to build community with others who are cultivating this new discipline of spiritual conversation that can aid us in the ability to discern what is best (Philippians 1:9-10).

In His Name,
Jeff Leis

HOW TO USE THIS STUDY GUIDE

Welcome to this 10-week study on *attitude*. We are excited to have you join us on a journey as we walk through the book of Philippians together and understand what the Apostle Paul teaches us about the impact of a healthy attitude. Each week of this study has eight sections that will stretch your understanding of Philippians and how a healthy attitude can reshape your perspective on life and build healthier, long-lasting relationships.

These uniquely crafted sections that are designed to stretch you along this journey include, **Devotionals, Memory Verses, Attitude Check, Group Observations, Life Applications, Kids & Adults Discussion, Practice Sessions** and **SOAP exercises**— all of which, are designed to correlate with each of the 10 weekend messages. By following this study guide, you will have many opportunities to grow spiritually through personal study (connecting with God), small group discussions (growing together with others), as well as critical discussion time with your mentees, children and more.

The *good news* is that you don't have to complete every section of this study. The *great news* is that it is very likely you will grow abundantly more if you embrace everything this study has to offer. We want to challenge you (in a good way) to not only show up for weekend services and engage in a small group study, but to also embrace one or more of the following challenges over the next 10 weeks:

Challenge #1
Memorize weekly memory verses.

Challenge #2
Engage in weekly practice sessions.

Challenge #3
SOAP weekly scriptures as scheduled (see instructions on page 8).

The Ultimate Challenge
All of the above! Memorize weekly memory verses, do the weekly practice sessions and keep a SOAP Journal.

HOW TO USE & UNDERSTAND EACH SECTION

1. **Devotionals** - These short story-like meditations will help you prepare for your small group discussion each week. We encourage everyone to read one or more of the devotionals for that week, and then dive into your memory verses and SOAP assignments.

2. Each week your group will have a **Memory Verse** from Philippians that applies to that week's lesson. Everyone is highly encouraged to meditate on and memorize each scripture during the week. You can find tips on page 11 that will give you memorization tools you can use for a lifetime.

3. During the **Attitude Check**, we mix it up a little by asking group or family members to share their personal experiences, and discuss various scenarios of how attitude shapes our reactions to circumstances in life.

4. In each **Group Observation**, you will be given sections of Philippians and supporting scriptures to read together and discuss with your group each week. You can read these during the week, or wait for your small group discussion. The group observation questions will facilitate discussion and insights into the section of Philippians that pertain to each week's topic.

5. In the **Life Application** section, each member of the group will share how the week's observations apply to their personal lives and choices. In this section, your group will explore different options to help them make better attitude choices.

6. **Kids & Adults** is a unique and fun opportunity to literally bring this study home to your family and mentoring relationships. The Kids & Adults section allows adults to have an observation time with their own kids, or other youth in their sphere of influence. We highly encourage everyone to engage children of all ages in this study.

7. **Practice Sessions** are designed to encourage you take it home and put each w week's principles into action.

8. **SOAP Exercises** - Your experience will be greatly enriched by using the SOAP method to further develop your understanding and application of Scripture throughout this study. Grab a journal and respond to each group of Scriptures by using the following acrostic on the next page (see SOAP schedule on page 9).

SOAP ACROSTIC

S = Scripture

Read the scripture and write it down in your journal, exactly as it is written.

O = Observation

What do you think the scripture is saying to the original hearers in the Bible? Do you see any principles, repeated words or concepts? Why do you think the author wrote what they did?

A = Application

How does the truth in this passage apply to me? Say it out loud. What could I do to live or think differently because of what this passage says?

P = Prayer

Pray for God to give you understanding of how He wants to use this scripture in your heart and life. Ask Him to help you to hear and understand His Holy Word. Quietly pause and listen. Ask Him to give you direction for the day, for the week, for your life. "Speak Lord. Your servant is listening!"

SOAP SCHEDULE

These SOAP assignments will also be located at the end of each week in this study guide. We encourage you to choose one or more of the weekly Scriptures in preparation for the next study. For example, SOAP the Scriptures during the week of your study and before the following week's message and small group.

Week 1
Philippians 1:3-6
Philippians 1:7-8
Philippians 1:9-11

Week 2
Philippians 1:27-30
Philippians 1:12-14
Philippians 1:15-18
Philippians 1:19-26

Week 3
Philippians 2:1-4
Ephesians 4:2-6
1 Peter 5:5-6

Week 4
Philippians 2:12-13
Philippians 2:14-18

Week 5
Philippians 4:9
Philippians 2:25-30
Philippians 2:19-24

Week 6
Philippians 4:4-7
James 1:2-4
Philippians 3:7-9

Week 7
Philippians 3:12-14
2 Corinthians 4:16-18
Philippians 3:20-21

Week 8
Philippians 4:11-13
Psalm 139:23-24
1 Thessalonians 5:16-18

Week 9
Philippians 4:10-13
2 Corinthians 12:9-10
Matthew 6:31-33

MEMORY VERSES

Theme verse
Philippians 2:5 *"Your attitude should be the same as that of Christ Jesus."*

Weeks 1 & 2
Philippians 1:6 *"Being confident of this, that he who began a good work in you will carry it on to completion until the day of Christ Jesus."*

Week 3
Philippians 1:27a *"Whatever happens, conduct yourselves in a manner worthy of the gospel of Christ."*

Weeks 4 & 5
Philippians 2:3-5 *"Do nothing out of selfish ambition or vain conceit, but in humility consider others better than yourselves. Each of you should look not only to your own interests, but also to the interests of others. Your attitude should be the same as that of Christ Jesus."*

Week 6
Philippians 4:9 *"What you have learned or received or heard from me, or seen in me—put it into practice. And the God of peace will be with you."*

Weeks 7 & 8
Philippians 4:4-7 *"Rejoice in the Lord always. I will say it again: Rejoice! Let your gentleness be evident to all. The Lord is near. Do not be anxious about anything, but in everything, by prayer and petition, with thanksgiving, present your requests to God. And the peace of God, which transcends all understanding, will guard your hearts and your minds in Christ Jesus."*

Week 9
Philippians 4:11b-13 *"I have learned to be content whatever the circumstances. I know what it is to be in need, and I know what it is to have plenty. I have learned the secret of being content in any and every situation, whether well fed or hungry, whether living in plenty or in want. I can do all this through him who gives me strength."*

Weeks 10
Review all of the memory verses from this study.

TIPS FOR MEMORIZATION

Memorization is the result of meditation. Meditation is creating space in your daily life to focus your heart and thoughts on God's word/truth. This is an important habit for transforming our minds in Christ Jesus (Romans 12:2).

Included are a few tips that will help you successfully memorize the Scriptures for this study, and hopefully throughout your lifetime. You are challenged to try the following techniques and learn these quick and easy tools for memorization:

1. Find a quiet place away from distractions to slowly read and think about each passage.

2. Focus on one phrase at a time and think about the meaning of each word and phrase.

3. Break the Scripture down into phrases and read each phrase out loud a minimum of 5 times. Then move on to the next phrase and repeat this process.

4. Read it with voice inflection, meaning and passion or create a melody to go along with the Scripture.

5. Practice your memorization with a family member or friend throughout the week. Review these steps daily until you confidently have it memorized.

INTRODUCTION

Thirty years ago, a dear friend of mine shared an experience that she had at the college she was attending. The story has never left me and often inspires me to evaluate my own attitude. It was basketball season. If you are a basketball fan, you know that a good competitive game can bring out the best in its players and sometimes the worst in its fans.

That was exactly the case at Northwest Nazarene University, a small Christian school in Nampa, Idaho. The game was already intense because the two teams were well matched, it was late in the season, the stakes were high, and they were arch rivals within their division.

As the score teetered back and forth, the NNU community was getting more and more spirited in their attitude; their volume and comments to the opposing team increasingly vitriolic. Eric Ely, the NNU center, a senior and a well known personality on campus, was becoming particularly annoyed by the toxic nature of the rising rhetoric. In an unprecedented maneuver, Eric with ball in hand, stops mid court, turns to his NNU family and yells correctively to the audience, "ATTITUDE CHECK!"

The bleachers fell silent as the stunned fans wrestled with what to do about the conundrum before them. Do they ignore the public rebuke of a beloved player and continue to feed their own flesh by justifying that it's "just a game?" They can behave any way they like... it's not real life, right? Or perhaps, they can recognize that their own attitudes were being flooded with natural adrenaline but not spiritual control, and take the admonition serious; make an attitudinal adjustment and appreciate the challenge to not just enjoy a great game but also make a greater witness to their faith.

What came next from the once fiery fans was maybe as surprising as Eric's own unconventional charge to them. Eric, who is enthusiastic about his faith, had been wearing sock extensions that had the phrase "Praise the Lord" printed on them. There was no doubt that his life, relationships and performance on the basketball court was dedicated to praising his Savior.

Momentum resumed in the game and so did the emotions and passion from the school's constituents. As tensions began to rise, Eric sent his message once more - "ATTITUDE CHECK!" As if someone secretly choreographed a planned response from the belly of the bleachers, came an enthusiastic, "PRAISE THE LORD!" Before long the majority of those in attendance were joining the volly, "ATTITUDE CHECK...PRAISE THE LORD!" What was on the verge of an emotionally explosive evening turned into a spiritually motivational event.

For weeks to come at almost every game, Eric and the NNU fans sent a message about their desired posture and sometimes fragile need to be reminded that our *attitude* needs to be *checked*.

A lesson was given and the message received. We are in charge of our attitudes. No one forces us, or makes us behave poorly. It is our choice how we will respond to life's challenges—the bad calls that are made, the fouls that are incurred, the missed opportunities, the shots that are blocked and the errors that are logged.

Nothing in life can bench us faster that our own toxic attitude; our own refusal to listen to a conversation going on—often within ourselves—and make a necessary attitude check and adjustment.

On that salient evening at Northwest Nazarene University, Eric instigated a conversation with a whole bleacher full of fans. That conversation could have gone a number of different directions. But the fans made a choice, they listened, and were humble enough to receive a message of truth from a messenger of love - attitude check!

Throughout the pages that will follow are a series of stories, scriptural meditations, antidotes, idioms and musings that have motivated me on countless days and innumerable moments to have a conversation about my attitude. I believe that an attitude check is as critical to a healthy faith as a physical exercise is to a healthy life.

I believe that every aberrant attitude can be changed by a conversation, and will most generally fail to be changed without a conversation. The powerful truth that I hope will be embraced at the onset of this study and then practiced throughout the study, is that you have the controls in your hands. You are the one who has the most power in your life to instigate the conversation that is needed for an attitude adjustment.

This conversation has three practical applications that every person who has learned to master their attitude knows how to instigate...*a conversation with themselves, a conversation with God, and a conversation with others.*

At its most basic level this critical conversation begins with you. You are constantly talking to yourself, but your awareness of what you are telling yourself ebbs and flows. You can occasionally catch what you are thinking, ruminating on or obsessing over, but usually you are unaware of the path your thoughts are taking you until you end up somewhere you mentally don't want to be - all of which are internal conversations. What if you could learn to better manage, catch and correct your unhealthy mental messages that sour your spirit and negatively alter your attitude?

Prayer is our most neglected spiritual weapon. Unaware of the devil's schemes we remain neutralized by our spiritual inactivity. In order to demolish the types of spiritual attacks, messages and assaults that the enemy wants to use against us, we must learn to have a continuous conversation with Christ's indwelling Spirit. Christ's power within us is so potent and yet remains so innocuous because of our inattention to His Word and His voice. What if you became utterly convinced of Christ's unconditional love and presence, so much so, that you intuitively began to reach for Him in your thoughts and decisions more quickly and naturally than any other instinct. Your attitude would be transformed.

A bad or sour attitude is often exacerbated by the conversations we have with others. We often declare that someone has set us off, pushed our buttons, or made us angry. Rather than learn to be an ambassador of a Christ-like attitude, we blame, accuse, and rifle others into being responsible for our own poor attitudes. What if you could cultivate the skills and insights necessary to never be taken captive by anyone else's attitude again, but rather discover how God wants to use you to set the tone of a Christ-like perspective, instead of succumbing to the tone of a Christ-less world?

You are not born with a good attitude. You can't go in your room and find a good attitude and you certainly don't stumble upon a good attitude. Your ability to master your attitude is directly related to your surrender to, and intimacy with, your Master Jesus Christ. Attitude is one's frame of mind that affects their disposition in life and the relationships around them. Please join us as we study the book of Philippians and discover how Christ's presence in us, not only brings us life, but also brings life to others through the power of a Christ-like attitude.

WEEK ONE

THE ORIGIN OF ATTITUDE

THIS WEEK'S THEME.

What is Attitude? In this week's material we want to accomplish two things: (1) Define "Attitude" from a Biblical perspective and refine it from a practical perspective; and (2) review the backdrop of the book of Philippians and the people who first formed this growing church. From this, we will see an eclectic group of people who found a common reason to begin meeting and growing in their faith, and how Paul's attitude led the way for God to shine into the lives of the new believers.

Take a group photo!

Post it to Facebook, Instagram or Twitter with the hashtag

#ATTITUDE

be sure to tag Yosemite Church!

Then print and glue your photo below.

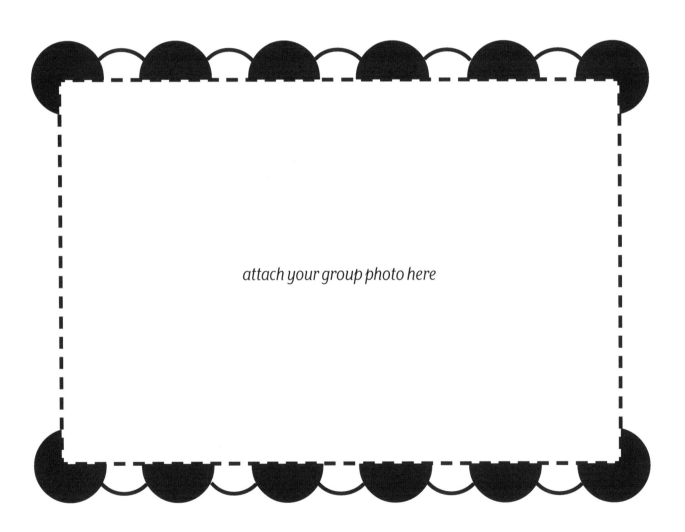

attach your group photo here

Take a few minutes to write what you would like to gain from this study.

_____

_____

_____

_____

_____

_____

_____

_____

_____

_____

_____

_____

_____

ORIGIN

Attitude. Everyone has one. Most of us struggle to control them. Few of us understand them. When we struggle with a negative attitude, we want to believe that others are probably to blame. *It's their fault, not mine! They have said or done the wrong thing, not me.* In fact, we have been overlooked, patronized, ignored, belittled or forgotten. We hate when people push our buttons; they don't even have the decency to consult, consider, or ask us our thoughts or opinions. We seldom stop to consider that maybe, just maybe, our attitude could impact how we react to the perceived offense.

Attitude. Every parent knows just how volatile a toddler's attitude can be. Without warning, their unmet fragile expectations can trigger meltdowns—taking us hostage in an instant. We can all empathize with panicked parents who want to escape to the nearest exit where they can unleash an appropriate reprimand on their pint-sized social terrorist in private.

Attitude. Where does it come from? Where does it go? How do we get a bad attitude and how do we keep a good one? Is it choice, is it heredity, or part of our personality? Is it nurture or nature?

Our study of the book of Philippians will take us on a spiritual journey to answer these questions and more. As we dig into this amazing New Testament book, we will find ourselves face-to-face with new insights as to the origins and power of attitude. We will discover how God packed this small letter to the Philippian Church with some incredibly important instructions on how to improve our personal attitude by taking on the attitude of Christ.

Attitude is one of the most critical elements for happiness and peace and yet, it's often the least developed skill in our spiritual tool box. This is partly because we perceive our attitude and emotions to be one and the same. Therefore, our emotional response can appear to be something out of our control; something that happens **to us** instead of **by us.**

What if our mental and spiritual disposition was something that aided us in our ability to choose an appropriate response instead of something that fueled and ignited an inappropriate reaction? What would change in our family gatherings, businesses, neighborhoods, board meetings, churches and social networks if we were better equipped to choose the best attitude? Our best attitude would better prepare us to face the challenges of each day, rather than falling victim to our own or someone else's bad behavior.

Most of us know the familiar feeling of being held captive - "walking on eggshells" - because of someone's toxic attitude. Would you be shocked if others thought that of you? We can detect quickly when we're the victim, but how about when we're the perpetrator? What if we could liberate ourselves from both sides of the equation?

Charles Swindoll captured the critical shift necessary to get a grip on one's attitude:

"The longer I live, the more I realize the impact of attitude on life. Attitude, to me, is more important than facts. It is more important than the past, than education, than money, than circumstances, than failures, than successes, than what other people think or say or do. It is more important than appearance, giftedness, or skill. It will make or break a company

... a church ... a home. The remarkable thing is we have a choice every day regarding the attitude we will embrace for that day. We cannot change the inevitable. The only thing we can do is play on the one string we have, and that is our attitude ... I am convinced that life is 10% what happens to me, and 90% how I react to it. And so it is with you ... we are in charge of our attitudes."

We can probably all agree, that this is easier said than done. Let us therefore seek as much biblical truth and spiritual insight as possible to grow in our competence to navigate the troubled waters from those inevitable attitude-related storms that will come our way.

Note from the author: As you work through the this study, inspired from the New Testament book of Philippians, I want you to know that I am excited! I believe, at the core of who we are as Jesus followers/disciples, we get better when we align our hearts with clear instruction from God's Word on how to be more like Him.

My prayer is that these devotional thoughts will take you higher; lifting you to perspectives that are above the fray of our troubled world and inspire you to adjust your mental focus to one that finds its origin in Jesus and His Spirit. When this shift happens in us, we are acutely aware that attitude is everyone's job. We cannot delegate attitude; assign it, force it, demand it or manipulate it. What we can do, is seek to model and mentor it. We can challenge one another to refuse to expect things from others that can only be done by each of us; to choose our attitude in any given situation.

How we do what we do is more important than what we do. Your ability determines what you can do. Your motivation determines what you will do. But your attitude determines how well you will do it. Zig Zigler said: *"Your attitude, not your aptitude, determines your altitude."*

A CIRCUMSTANTIAL ATTITUDE

Philippians 2:5 *"Your attitude should be the same as that of Christ Jesus."*

When we believe that God speaks through the scriptures, we expect Him to reveal things to us we either do not know, or do not understand. Comprehension should always be the first step of our goal; that we would understand what the Spirit wants to show us, where he wants to lead us, and how he wants to transform us. That is the understanding I am referring to. It is what Paul was praying for in Philippians 1:9, *"I pray that your love may abound more and more in knowledge and depth of insight, so that you may be able to discern what is best, and may be pure and blameless for the day of Christ."* That's not just comprehension, that's transformation! When we have an attitude like Christ (Philippians 2:5), it's not a white knuckle, stiff upper lip, pushing our way through the difficulties of life attitude; it's something much more relaxed that can't be manufactured by our human resolve.

The transformational attitude that we will grow to develop will lead us through many ups and downs. We will wind our way through misbeliefs, misunderstandings and missed opportunities. The change we long for does not come to us in a single moment, it comes in the journey.

When we read and begin to fathom the story of the apostle Paul and His personal encounter with Jesus, we discover that God always wants to transform. To have an attitude like Christ wasn't a far-fetched idea of some over-the-top Jesus enthusiast. Instead, it was the reality of knowing Jesus more deeply as the One who takes up residence in us and lovingly fills us with Himself.

Our attitude is as much caught as it is taught (Philippians 3:17 & 4:9). It is less about trying and more about training (Philippians 4:11-12). Paul wasn't trying to give the Philippians a spiritual pep talk. He was inviting them into a daily walk with Jesus and other mature believers that would empower them to experience Him at an intensely intimate and vulnerable level.

> "Attitude, not aptitude will determine your altitude."
> -Zig Zigler

When it comes to our attitude, most of us are very circumstantial. In other words, if our circumstances are good, our attitude has a high potential of also being good. Conversely, if our circumstances are bad, our attitude is bad or at least teetering on the edge of bad. That isn't the attitude of Jesus. His attitude is never circumstantial.

While we are on this journey, what if you discover how to employ a Christ-like attitude? What if you learn to be empowered in God's presence; to see your circumstances through His eyes? Ultimately, that is what alters our attitude. We must learn to shift ourselves away from our circumstantial perspective, and focus on God's supernatural perspective. That is exactly what happened to the apostle Paul, and it can happen for us.

A Christ-like attitude is an attitude from a different altitude. It's a higher perspective—one that sees from God's vantage point.

On many occasions, I have suffered from low attitude that was in direct proportion to a low altitude. I couldn't see the forest through the trees. I was so deep in the mess, all I could see was the mess. My lack of objectivity buried my perspective so deep that I couldn't even imagine how God was, or could be working.

For the apostle Paul, it was mind over matter. His altitude was critical for attitude to change. He lived and breathed a higher perspective. He learned a skill that empowered him to abandon an earthly perspective and exchange it with the higher perspective found in Jesus. That higher perspective is for all of us. In Colossians 3:1-2, Paul asserts, *"since then you have been raised with Christ, set your hearts on things above, where Christ is seated at the right hand of God. Set your mind on things above, not on earthly things."*

We cannot control the circumstances of life, but we can control our attitudes toward those circumstances. Life can and will throw us a curveball. The question is always - what will we do with it? When we expect life to go our way and serve up wonderful opportunities, we will inevitably miss the miracle that God promises to those who believe. He can work amidst the worst of circumstances to bring the greatest opportunities. You have an opportunity before you today, to embrace a higher perspective. Whatever your circumstances may be, take a moment and set your heart, your mind, your affections and attention on Christ.

Instead of trying to get out of your situation, ask the Spirit to reveal what he wants you to get out of your situation. Is there something he is wanting to do in your spirit to reflect His presence? Is there something he wants you to learn that you've been avoiding? Is there a hurt, a wound or a fear that he may be asking you to face and turn over to him? When we believe deeply that God is at work, we are given the opportunity to discover where and what he is doing. That discovery is either enabled or disabled by our attitude.

MEMORY VERSE

Philippians 1:6
"Being confident of this, that he who began a good work in you will carry it to completion until the day of Christ Jesus."

THE ORIGIN OF ATTITUDE

OPEN IN PRAYER. After opening in prayer, take some time to connect with your group. If there are newcomers, let them briefly share about themselves and how they came to your group.

Attitude Check. Go around the room and discuss what everyone's definition of attitude is. Ask them what they are hoping to get out of this study.

DIVING DEEPER

Attitude: One's frame of mind that affects their disposition in life and the relationships around them. *Phroneo* is the Greek word that is translated "attitude" in our English Bibles. *Phroneo*, or a form of this word, is used 11 times in Philippians. It can be translated: *adopt, view, concern, concerned, feel, have...attitude, live in harmony, mind, set their minds, set your mind* and *think*. Greek scholar J. Thayer points out that phoneo carries the idea of being able to *"properly regulate (moderate) from within, while inner-perspective (insight) shows itself in corresponding, outward behavior."*

Leaders:
Over the course of your small group study we want to encourage you to commit to memory several scriptures. There will not be a memory verse each week, but we ask that you give every one an opportunity to share a verse with the group or in pairs each week.

The Apostle Paul, after his conversion (Acts 9) and at a time of sequestered growth and development (Galatians 1:17-18), emerged back on the public scene as the Apostle to the Gentiles (Acts 26:17-18 & Galatians 1:15-16). This meant taking the gospel message to those outside the Jewish community and nation of Israel. For the rest of his life, he would dedicate himself to doing whatever was necessary to finish the work God had given him to do (Acts 20:24).

In our first week together, we drop in on the Apostle Paul and a few of his companions and mentees as they traveled into the region of Macedonia where Philippi is the leading city. Paul, in Acts 16, is called in a dream to go to Macedonia. There, he and his companions meet the first followers from Philippi; undoubtedly the beginnings of the community that would become the recipients of his letter to the Philippian Church.

Philippi being the "leading city" would have meant that it was the hub of a large metropolitan area where trade and commerce were the norm. It was a melting pot of ethnic people from all over the Roman empire — a perfect place to plant a church and watch the light of the gospel spread.

Leaders:
Please read through the Diving Deeper section. Choose one or more Options to process with your group.

Option 1
GROUP OBSERVATION

Take a few minutes and look up each of the following passages that use the word Phroneo. Notice what we are being asked to do in each passage and share your thoughts on how each use of the word might affect one's attitude—Philippians 2:5 & 4:10; Colossians 3:1-2; 1 Corinthians 1:10 & 2:16; 2 Corinthians 13:11; and Romans 12:2-3. After reading a few of the passages together, allow some time for a few members of your group to share their thoughts about the use of the word and its application to attitude.

Life Application: Either ask someone to share with the group, or break into pairs and share a time when you were struggling with your attitude and how that struggle affected your own mental health, or those around you. What kind of circumstances are the most difficult for you to navigate and rise above with a good attitude?

Option 2
GROUP OBSERVATION

Look over the sermon notes and ask someone to either read Acts 16 or give an overview of what takes place and the people that are introduced in this chapter. Ask the group to make some observations about each of the main characters in each experience and those who are the secondary characters. What was interesting about them? How did Paul's interaction with each one make an impact? What was Paul's attitude in each situation and how do you think his attitude contributed to the overall impact of those in the passage?

Life Application: Earlier, we read that people in the passage were from a diverse background - upper class, lower class, and middle class. What other differences do you see or could you imagine might have been present? What has your attitude been when it comes to being with people who are different then you? How important do you think it is for believers (Christ followers) to have a positive attitude toward other believers that are different from them ethnically, socially, economically, generationally, and culturally? Which of these differences are most challenging for you to have a positive attitude toward? How important is a spirit of inclusivity and how can we cultivate it in our church?

PRACTICE THIS WEEK. Choose one or two things you will apply from today's study and report back next week about how you were able to implement them.

SOAP ASSIGNMENT. Below are the Scriptures to SOAP this next week. If you have never done a SOAP exercise before, review the instructions located in the front of this Study Guide. During your small group time, consider having one or two people share their SOAP with the group, or pair-up and share with one other person.
- **Philippians 1:3-6**
- **Philippians 1:7-8**
- **Philippians 1:9-11**

Leaders:
Spend a few minutes in prayer before closing. Either pray together collectively or break into pairs. Try to practice some confession. Have everyone share areas where they see a weakness in their attitude. Pray for God to empower each of you to be of "one mind" and set your mind on things that will help you shift to a Christ-like attitude both personally and in your relationships.

KIDS & ADULTS

Ask your child, grandchild, or mentee a few of the following questions while you are together this week. What do they think *attitude* means? Ask them to describe and give an example of what a good attitude and a bad attitude might look like. If you feel courageous, ask them to describe a time when they have witnessed you having a bad attitude. This could be a very powerful way to show your children, grandchildren or mentee(s) that you are a *work in process* just like everyone else, and have the humility to illustrate that we can all make progress in our growth. The more you model a willingness to grow in your attitude, the more others will follow.

WEEK TWO

THE DIFFERENCE MAKER

THIS WEEK'S THEME.

This week, the gospel has the power to change our attitude - the difference the gospel can make. Remember that our attitude is a reflection of our "state of mind" and that we can each grow in our ability to set our mind on what God calls us to focus on, which can then influence and change our attitude in any given situation.

HOW WAS YOUR WEEK?

Have some fun and take some time to do a word
search based on Week 2.

Find these words

acceptance	affection	approval	attitude
change	confidence	difference	direction
disgust	encouraged	gospel	happiness
identity	Jesus	joy	lazy
participation	philippians	rejection	scorn
shame			

Once you're done give yourself a pat on the back!

ATTITUDE SEARCH

```
p c u z q k r b f h l w i q o j n a r g
k c l i c w y l b j q e s w v t p t x o
n y z a l f g n x n r q g x n l g a e p
a e j z v o r e j f j d j u b x u q o h
q d i s s o q x t g w c i r e g u l u i
z e x p c t r c x s h o j r o e s z g l
l o e s h f k p n a v w j c e n v f j i
c l t c a u n o p c u c y e u c n j w p
f t r p n k o p e a o s c d s o t y g p
f y i a g a i n p a j n h u i u b i m i
r r i d e n t i t y e z f t q r s n o a
k e y i e f c p a r t i c i p a t i o n
u z e s y q e u e v u e w t d g b o j s
a d s g z k f f e c j u m t q e u f r k
p y f u t t f z r e c o u a q d n p l c
a r r s c i a h r k c a y l h y r c z y
e b s t d k a y c d i z l d k s o k e f
```

THROUGH THE LENS OF THE GOSPEL

Attitudes don't change without a perspective change. Attending to Christ's presence and the influence of the Spirit of God within us has to be cultivated. That cultivation for the apostle Paul, at it's core, was the influence and impact of the gospel.

The gospel means *good news*. So if we have good news, there is hopefully an adjustment that comes with that good news. Just how powerful is the good news? It is as powerful as you cultivate it to be.

For the person who loves to read and I mean really loves to read - I'm not talking about the person that enjoys a good book while on vacation, I'm talking about the person who almost always has a book or their Kindle with them. At every opportunity, in every waiting room, break room, bathroom, living room, bedroom, they make room to read. For them, there are stories, mysteries, novels, biographies, tragedies and adventures that rest on shelves and are never more than a few steps or pages away from transporting them to another place through the captivating skill of a good writer. For the rest of us, those are unexplored adventures that may never come to life.

We read about the gospel all over the scriptures. You don't have to acquire a fetish for reading to enlarge your experience of the gospel. But you do have to cultivate a fetish for Jesus and the work he has accomplished, and is still accomplishing, to maximize the effect of the gospel on your perspective. Like an avid reader we have to fill every spare moment with a compulsion to see life through the lens of Jesus. The gospel has to saturate our mental space so much that good news becomes our default perspective.

One cannot read the New Testament and miss just how ubiquitous the gospel is. It is everywhere and for good reason. Not that we take it for granted but that we take it for gratitude. That is where the book of Philippians kicks off, on the heels of Paul's introduction. He jumps right into the gospel. Philippians 1:3-6 says, *"I thank my God every time I remember you. In all my prayers, for all of you, I always pray with joy because of your partnership in the **gospel** from the first day until now, being confident of this, that he who began a good work in you will carry it on to completion until the day of Christ."*

At the center of the New Testament is the gospel and at the center of the gospel is Jesus. Paul uses the Greek term *euaggelion*; eu = good + aggelio = proclaim or tell (the gospel). This term is used nine times in Philippians and 76 times in the New Testament. It became synonymous with Jesus and the work he was and still is doing.

Prior to Jesus, this word in secular Greek appears in two contexts: the common context and the imperial context. The *common context* is how it was used by the common people, then and today. One might ask, "Do you have any good news for me?" Why? This is because we all prefer good news over bad news. In the common context, good news always was (and still is) circumstantial. If you had good circumstances—a safe new birth of a child—it was good news. If you received a promotion and now make more money—more good news.

In the *imperial context*, euaggelion was used to describe the rule of Caesar Augustus, and the good news of peace he brought to the known world. The major difference between Caesar's peace and the peace of Christ, is the way it is achieved. For Caesar it was the power of his sword. For Jesus, it is the power of His love.

It is really quite amazing that the gospel Jesus brought to us has so dwarfed any notion from the imperial cult of Caesar, that there is no connection in the mind of the everyday person today to Caesar and his gospel. In contrast, the gospel introduced by Jesus is perceived by many as indigenous to Christianity. The good news is that all mankind can have access to God's grace and forgiveness; that God is for us and not against us, and has the power to change the mindset of anyone willing to make it the focus of their heart. It is what empowers the believer to set their minds on the good God has promised to do for all who love him.

Gratitude is the attitude of someone who sees life through the lens of the gospel—not because of their circumstances, but because of the confidence they have in God to work on their behalf regardless of their circumstances.

The gospel was at the core of what changed the apostle Paul's perspective of everything. In our journey through the book of Philippians, we will continue to reach out and take hold of the mindset that drove Paul to proclaim, *"Being confident of this, that He who began a good work in you will carry it on to completion until the day of Christ."*

An attitude of gratitude is one which finds its origin in the gospel of Jesus. If attitude is a choice, when we make the choice to have a different, or improved attitude, it becomes the difference-maker in turbulent circumstances. If attitude is that critical, then what empowers someone to embrace a better attitude? What might enable an average person to seize an above average attitude? The New Testament suggests that the difference-maker, for the believer, is the gospel. If we define attitude as a frame of mind that affects our disposition in life and the relationships around us, then how do we adopt a gospel frame of mind?

Early in my Christian walk I picked up a little aphorism that has repeatedly helped me to refine my attitude. *Sow a thought, reap an attitude. Sow an attitude, reap an action. Sow an action, reap a habit. Sow a habit, reap a character. Sow a character, reap a destiny.* The Bible says plainly, *"Do not be deceived, God cannot be mocked. A man reaps what he sows"* (Galatians 6:7). For no other reason, we should be motivated to sow what will most likely affect our destiny.

I have often prayed the classic prayer by St. Francis of Assisi to remind myself of the kind of thoughts and choices I want to sow.

Lord, make me an instrument of your peace:
where there is hatred, let me sow love;
where there is injury, let me sow pardon;
where there is doubt, let me sow faith;
where there is despair, let me sow hope;
where there is darkness, let me sow light;
where there is sadness, let me sow joy.

O divine Master, grant that I may not so much seek
to be consoled as to console,
to be understood as to understand,
to be loved as to love.
For it is in giving that we receive,
it is in pardoning that we are pardoned,
and it is in dying that we are born to eternal life.
Amen.

WHEN MY ATTITUDE BEGAN TO CHANGE

For many years, I struggled with a negative perception about myself. This began as a child in elementary school with an undiagnosed learning disorder that impaired my academic performance. We now refer to it as dyslexia – where you turn your letters and numbers around. I turned c-a-t into t-a-c and d-o-g into g-o-d, etc.

I did pretty well in school with the exception of reading, writing and arithmetic. Even when I was under the illusion (perception) that I had done something well, I was quickly jolted back to the reality of my perpetual inadequacy. I was a straight D student, with an occasional F thrown in, getting pushed through the system.

As a sophomore in high school, I was evaluated and can still remember the evaluator saying that, "he is only reading at a third grade level."

Because of this sour assessment, it was determined that I needed to be taken out of the mainstream class of my peers and be placed into a Special Ed program. This did not make me feel special! Every day of school, up to this point, was difficult at best, and often dreaded, but now it seemed unbearable. The stigma that I perceived convinced me that I was stupid, unwanted and worthless.

I had developed a whole set of skills to help hide my inadequacies but now I was exposed. I could no longer hide the fact that I was dumb. I know now that perception is not reality, but it sure felt like it at the time.

"He who began a good work in you will carry it on to completion."
Philippians 1:6

As a teenager, my brother and I attended a small country church with some neighbors. That summer they held a week of meetings for the youth and on the final night, they gave an invitation to accept a relationship with Christ.

I learned that there would be another evaluation that would determine our eternal destiny. But this evaluation was different. The critical issue was not going to be about something I had done, but rather what Jesus had done for me. There would not be a series of questions that I would answer to determine or prove how capable I was to earn my acceptance, but rather one question to determine if I had received the acceptance that Jesus won for me on the cross.

I learned that we all struggle from a learning disorder called sin that impairs our judgment and distorts our perceptions. It can cause us to think we are the best one moment, and the worst the next. It tricks us into thinking that we can be prideful, selfish and arrogant and it's OK. It convinces us that even though deep down we are insecure, afraid and anxious, the only thing worse, is someone else knowing it. So we hide those things hoping somehow we'll get better.

That night, I gave my heart to Jesus and I asked Him to come and live in mine. I received the love, acceptance and forgiveness that Jesus won for me when He died on the cross. In that magical moment my attitude (my frame of mind) began to change.

I have had a lot of ups and downs over the years, but the love and acceptance—the purpose and meaning that I now have as a child of God—is not only what I enjoy every day, but it is also what I am committed to share with others. When Jesus entered my heart— when His Spirit moved in—everything began to change. He who began that good work in me, is still at work, and will bring to completion his purposes.

I am utterly convinced that what He has done, and what He is doing in me, He will do in you. If you have not yet opened your heart to Him, do it now. Let Him fill you with His Spirit who is waiting to affirm you as a child of God. When you do, everything will begin to change.

MEMORY VERSE

Philippians 1:6
"Being confident of this, that he who began a good work in you will carry it to completion until the day of Christ Jesus."

THE DIFFERENCE MAKER

OPEN IN PRAYER. Get comfortable with the idea of practicing gratitude (a huge way to improve one's attitude). Go around the room and share a short sentence of gratitude, or pair up with another member of the group and each share (in prayer) something you are grateful for.

Attitude Check. Review the practice session from last week. Have everyone share their experience. Now, break into groups of three and ask each group to brainstorm as many "Difference Makers" that they can think of in sports, technology, business, faith, etc. For example, Michael Jordan was a difference maker in basketball.

Pull the groups back together and share some of their "Difference Makers". Then ask what or how each thing or person made such a difference? (e.g., with Michael Jordan he performed at a higher level - more scoring and rebounds than other players).

DIVING DEEPER

So, if the gospel is "good news" for the believer, what difference does it make? Look at each passage below and process with your group, mentee or child what difference the gospel makes according to each passage.

Romans 1:16-17 *"For I am not ashamed of the gospel, because it is the power of God that brings salvation to everyone who believes: first to the Jew, then to the Gentile. For in the gospel the righteousness of God is revealed—a righteousness that is by faith from first to last, just as it is written: 'The righteous will live by faith.'"*

Leaders:
If members in your group are engaging in the Kids & Adults section, briefly ask them how the weekly time with their children, or mentee is going. We want to be more assertive with involving our kids in spiritual conversations. Making this a part of your review will help cultivate and strengthen this church-wide goal.

1 Corinthians 15:1-4 *"Now, brothers and sisters, I want to remind you of the gospel I preached to you, which you received and on which you have taken your stand. By this gospel you are saved, if you hold firmly to the word I preached to you. Otherwise, you have believed in vain. For what I received I passed on to you as of first importance: that Christ died for our sins according to the Scriptures, that he was buried, that he was raised on the third day according to the Scriptures."*

How do the Scriptures you just read affirm that Jesus died for our sins and then rose from the dead to show us that he was God? What difference does Christ's death and resurrection make?

Because of God's good news (the gospel), we now have several things that are true for everyone who believes in and puts their trust in Jesus.

Leaders:
Pick one or more of the following options to process with your group. Have your group members consider processing one or more of these sections with a youth in their sphere of influence this week.

Option 1

ur identification with Jesus changes our identity.

Philippians 1:1 *"Paul and Timothy, servants of Christ Jesus, To all God's holy people in Christ Jesus at Philippi, together with the overseers and deacons."*

Life Application: Consider how your spiritual identity is being established as you reflect on the following questions:

A. How is Jesus (the gospel) changing how you see yourself - who you are?

B. Which side of the two lists describe more how you see yourself?

Unwanted	Wanted
Child of man	Child of God
Insignificant	Significant
Rejected	Accepted
Performance	Relationship
Worried about life	At peace in life
Stressed	Relaxed

C. What kind of difference would it make in your relationships if you began to see yourself more consistently like God sees you?

Option 2

ur participation in the gospel (the message of Jesus).

In the following Scriptures, how did the Philippian believers help in the spread of the gospel?

Philippians 1:3-6 *"I thank my God every time I remember you. In all my prayers for all of you, I always pray with joy because of your partnership in the gospel from the first day until now, being confident of this, that he who began a good work in you will carry it on to completion until the day of Christ Jesus."*

Philippians 4:15-16 *"Moreover, as you Philippians know, in the early days of your acquaintance with the gospel, when I set out from Macedonia, not one church shared with me in the matter of giving and receiving, except you only; for even when I was in Thessalonica, you sent me aid more than once when I was in need."*

Philippians 1:27-30 *"Whatever happens, conduct yourselves in a manner worthy of the gospel of Christ. Then, whether I come and see you or only hear about you in my absence, I will know that you stand firm in the one Spirit, striving together as one for the faith of the gospel without being frightened in any way by those who oppose you. This is a sign to them that they will be destroyed, but that you will be saved—and that by God. For it has been granted to you on behalf of Christ not only to believe in him, but also to suffer for him, since you are going through the same struggle you saw I had, and now hear that I still have."*

GROUP OBSERVATION

Life Application: What can you apply from these Scriptures that will help you spread the gospel in your community?

Option 3

ur affections for others through Jesus.

GROUP OBSERVATION

Based on what we have studied so far, and the following verses, why and how has Paul expressed his affection for the believers in Philippi?

Philippians 1:7-8 *"It is right for me to feel this way about all of you, since I have you in my heart and, whether I am in chains or defending and confirming the gospel, all of you share in God's grace with me. God can testify how I long for all of you with the affection of Christ Jesus."*

Life Application: How have you developed affection for others because of the gospel? What difference does Jesus make in your ability to have an affectionate attitude toward others?

Option 4

ur direction in life because of Jesus

Jesus changing our direction in life is an understatement for those who know and love him deeply. In the new church of Philippi, we saw how three lives were impacted and changed (Lydia, the slave girl and the jailer). In this section, we also see Paul praying for continued change. How was Paul's own story an example of ongoing change? In the group observation and life application sections, consider how the gospel continues to change our direction in life.

GROUP OBSERVATION

How does Paul's prayer in verses 9-11 below illustrate what needs to happen for Jesus' influence over us to impact the direction of our life?

Philippians 1:9-11 *"And this is my prayer: that your love may abound more and more in knowledge and depth of insight, so that you may be able to discern what is best and may be pure and blameless for the day of Christ, filled with the fruit of righteousness that comes through Jesus Christ—to the glory and praise of God."*

Life Application: How would a deeper grasp of God's love improve your discernment? What effect might that have on your direction in life from day to day?

PRACTICE THIS WEEK. Choose one or two things you will apply from today's study and report back next week about how you were able to implement the application.

SOAP ASSIGNMENT. Below are the Scriptures to SOAP this next week. If you have never done a SOAP exercise before, review the instructions located in the front of this Study Guide. During your small group time, consider having one or two people share their SOAP with the group, or pair-up and share with one other person.
- **Philippians 1:27-30**
- **Philippians 1:12-14**
- **Philippians 1:15-18**
- **Philippians 1:19-26**

Leaders:

Encourage your group to do the practice section for this week. Spend a few minutes in prayer before closing. Either pray together collectively or break into pairs. Try to practice some confession. Have everyone share areas where they see a weakness in their attitude. Pray for God to empower each of you to be of "one mind" and set your mind on things that will help you shift to a Christ-like attitude, personally and in your relationships.

KIDS & ADULTS Ask your child, grandchild, or mentee a few of the following questions while you are gathered together. Remind them that the gospel means "good news" and it is all about what Jesus has done for us. **Observation: What is some good news that you are excited about or have heard at school or home? Why do you think the Bible calls what Jesus did for us "good news"?**

WEEK THREE

BENEFITS OF A CHRIST-LIKE ATTITUDE

THIS WEEK'S THEME.

The power of attitude when times are tough.

A Christ-like attitude is the attitude we are seeking to understand and learning to employ as we walk together through this season. In the second half of Philippians 1:12-30 there are multiple indicators that this spiritual ability, to choose the higher Christ-centered attitude, has multiple benefits, especially when times are tough.

HOW WAS YOUR WEEK?

Choose Your Own Attitude

Groggily you roll out of bed. After pushing your snooze button three times you can't possibly make it to work on time if you stay there. You stumble into the bathroom and turn on the shower and the warm water revives you. You reach for the body wash only to find that the bottle is empty. You...

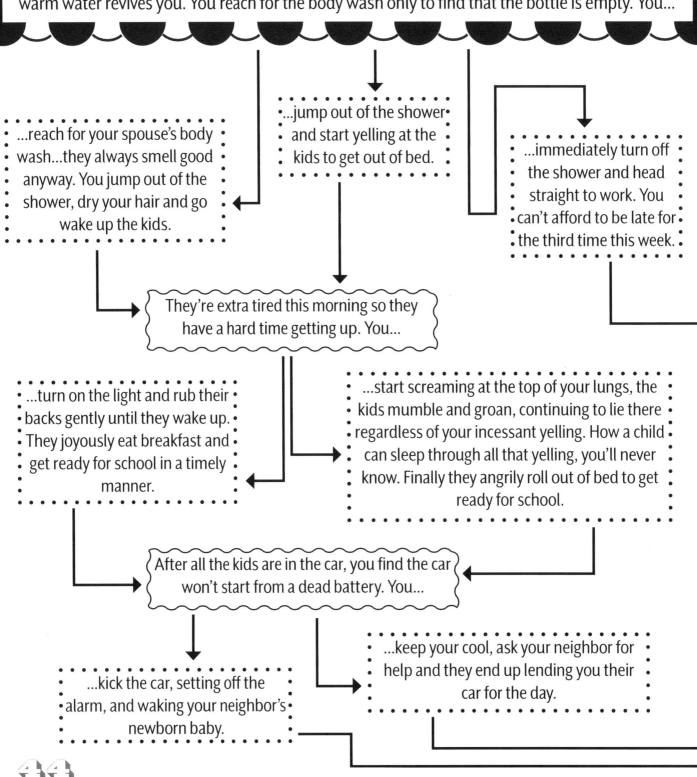

...reach for your spouse's body wash...they always smell good anyway. You jump out of the shower, dry your hair and go wake up the kids.

...jump out of the shower and start yelling at the kids to get out of bed.

...immediately turn off the shower and head straight to work. You can't afford to be late for the third time this week.

They're extra tired this morning so they have a hard time getting up. You...

...turn on the light and rub their backs gently until they wake up. They joyously eat breakfast and get ready for school in a timely manner.

...start screaming at the top of your lungs, the kids mumble and groan, continuing to lie there regardless of your incessant yelling. How a child can sleep through all that yelling, you'll never know. Finally they angrily roll out of bed to get ready for school.

After all the kids are in the car, you find the car won't start from a dead battery. You...

...kick the car, setting off the alarm, and waking your neighbor's newborn baby.

...keep your cool, ask your neighbor for help and they end up lending you their car for the day.

On your way to the work you hit EVERY. RED. LIGHT. You realize that you left the kids in their beds asleep. On your way back home you run a red light. You hear the sirens and see the lights in your review mirror. You...

...accept getting pulled over.

...run from the cops.

Even though you've had setbacks, you still manage to make it to work on time. But you forget about an important meeting and your boss calls you into their office. You...

You embark on a high speed chase which somehow ends in your grandma breaking her hip, you getting the same issue of Cat Lovers magazine for 5 years, and finally getting sucked into a black hole.

...apologize and offer to work late.

...you blame your coworker, Jeremiah, for spilling coffee on your computer, making it impossible for you to access your calendar.

YOU LOSE!!
Your attitude stinks like dead fish rotting on the wharf. You end up doing all of Jeremiah's smelly, moist laundry for a year.

YOU WIN!!
Look at you, you winner! Hot dog! Ain't nothin' holding you down! When things don't go your way, you take it in stride and manage to keep everyone around you happy too. Keep on keepin' on!

DISNEYFICATION

Disneyfied; yes that really is a word. It is what happens when a society, business, or perspective has been altered to resemble the theme park Disneyland. I have several friends who are absolute Disney enthusiasts. They have hundreds of Disney trinkets and dozens of clothes that display all the characters and symbols of Disneyland. They frequent the park more than most of us frequent the mall.

There is nothing wrong with that. I love the Magic Kingdom as much as the next guy. The issue isn't about a place where every conceivable attempt has been made, through an enormous amount of money spent, with the highest level of training imaginable, to craft an environment where people can escape into an artificial world. Rather, it is the misbelief or mythical thinking that such a world could become our reality.

"For it has been granted to you on behalf of Christ not only to believe in him, but also to suffer for him."
Philippians 1:29

In the life of every person there is a deep need to understand suffering and trials, which isn't built into the experience of the Magic Kingdom. This key area of growth can empower every person to move from an attitude of defeat and disappointment to one of adventure and victory. When we resist learning this spiritual truth, ultimately, we sabotage our own spiritual development.

What happens in times of difficulty is potentially the greatest indicator of genuine faith and commitment. Most of us have fallen into mythical thinking that suggests life is at its best when all is well; when there are no adversities, no conflicts and no shortages. Unfortunately, no one lives in that space longer than a day or two, or perhaps a long weekend. Eventually, we all have to leave the brilliant colors of perfectly manicured flower beds, fairies zipping across the sky, castles dominating the skyline and perfect customer service, to our own less-than-perfect homes, yards, jobs and lives.

What if the real adventure lies not in the perfect but the imperfect, not in the ideal but the real, not in the flawless but the flawed. What if God's most powerful work and the greatest display of His presence is brought to life when we learn to love the unlovely, to remember the forgotten, embrace the broken, or champion a spirit of trust and faith in the midst of life's trials? I believe that is the message in Philippians 1:12-30. Paul is living out his own philosophy of life and ministry and inviting the reader to join him.

WHY ME LORD?

How do you handle a bad day? Have you ever asked, "Why me Lord - what have I ever done?" Did you ever hear someone say, "I am just waiting for the other shoe to drop" or "What else could possibly go wrong?" Sometimes we feel stuck in a *comedy of errors.*

I have had those days when it seems like everything that could go wrong, goes wrong. Your alarm doesn't go off (or if it did, you turned it off and fell back to sleep). You're now late for an important meeting at your new job and none of your shirts seem to fit, look good, are clean, or ironed. You grab a cup of microwaved coffee, burn your tongue on the way out the door, and then realize, as you jump in your car, you left your cup on the roof while juggling everything you were trying to throw in the front seat.

Now there is a broken cup in the front of your driveway. You look down and your gas gauge is on empty—the light's even on. While praying that you can just make it to work, it seems like every single light in the universe is red. You've never realized how stinking long these lights stay red! You back up and drive forward because you're sure the light sensor must have missed you pulling up. On your second back and forth attempt, you slam into another driver behind you. He's upset and insists on calling the police. You can't find your insurance card and just realized that your wallet's on the kitchen counter next to the microwave. Everything that could go wrong...

Struggles, trials, difficulties, problems and hardship are never invited guests, but rather unwelcome intruders. We find them lurking in our homes— bumping into them at every intersection—sleeping in our bed, living in our house and working with us on our jobs. We can feel like we've been hexed by a curse, or are being punished for some act of disobedience.

This is when our attitudes are the most fragile; when we are nearing an emotional explosion, a mental meltdown or a full blown relapse into a two-year-old tantrum. Now, as you experience the collapse of what you thought was a potentially good day, everything is susceptible to getting even worse. WAIT! How could things get any worse?

Let's look at how BAD can go to WORSE...

Your alarm doesn't go off, so you throw it across the room. It hits and breaks the dresser mirror into hundreds of pieces on the floor. You're now late for an important meeting at your new job and none of your shirts seem to fit, look good, are clean, or ironed. You step on the broken mirror and cut your bare feet. After putting on four band-aids you head to the kitchen, grab a cup of microwaved coffee and burn your tongue on the first sip. You're so mad you kick the dog who then runs through the house peeing on the floor.

As you jump in your car, you realize you left your coffee cup on the roof. While driving away you see your neighbor, right behind you, drive over the broken coffee cup and puncture his tire. He's now out of his car yelling at you as you drive away. Pretending not to see him, you just keep going. You look down and your gas gauge is on empty.

While praying that you can just make it to work it seems like every single light in the universe is red. You back up and drive forward because you're sure the light sensor must have missed you. On your second back and forth attempt you slam into another driver behind you. He's upset, insisting on calling the police. You can't find your insurance card and just realize that your wallet's on the kitchen counter next to the microwave.

You snap at the driver; telling him he's an idiot for wanting to call the police. He reacts, gets in your face and you shove him away. Now he's threatening to sue you. Furious, you jump in your car, speed off, swearing at him, and roll down your window to give him an unfriendly hand sign. You get about half a block away and your car sputters to a stop because you're out of gas. Your neighbor pulls up next to you in his wife's car, still screaming. You see the other driver walking toward you in the rear view mirror and hear a police siren as a patrol car pulls around the corner. Things can get worse, and they usually do when our attitude becomes part of the problem instead of rising above it.

It seems like everything that could go wrong, goes wrong.

In the first chapter of Philippians we hear Paul, who is in chains in a Roman prison, refuse to allow his attitude to become part of the problem. Instead, he enumerates all of the advantages and benefits to living out his relationship with Christ in the midst of suffering. His attitude literally turns his suffering into cause for rejoicing. After praying for the Philippians, he starts his list of reasons to rise above his difficulties.

- Vs 12 *"Now I want you to know, brothers, that what has happened to me has really served to **advance the gospel.**"*

- Vs 13 *"As a result, **it has become clear** throughout the whole palace guard and to everyone else that **I am in chains for Christ.**"*

- Vs 14 *"**Because of my chains,** most of the brothers in the Lord have been encouraged to speak the word of God **more courageously and fearlessly.**"*

I would wager that things could get worse. And, they usually do when our attitude adds insult to injury. When our frame of mind is set on the expectation that bad things shouldn't happen to good people, we set ourselves up for a disconnect from reality. For Paul, in this Roman prison and for you and I, when we allow God into our suffering and difficulties, (not to alleviate them, but to be present in them with us), we discover a new and different capacity for dealing with our difficulties. When we fail to realize that the God who is in us wants to show up and be seen in all of our difficulties, the power of who Christ is gets lost in the midst of the suffering and challenges.

No matter what you are going through, the Spirit of God wants to comfort, encourage, refine, and be seen in you. This is where God's grace comes to live within us at a deeper level; where we discover Jesus in the dark night, in the unanswered prayer and in the difficulties and obstacles of life.

Kris Kristofferson's Country and Western hit song in the early 1970's "Why me, Lord?" expressed this attitude shift that puts us back in a place of spiritual dependence instead of independence, of resting instead of resistance, and of praising instead of pining.

Why me Lord, what have I ever done
To deserve even one
Of the pleasures I've known
Tell me Lord, what did I ever do
That was worth loving you

Or the kindness you've shown.
Lord help me Jesus, I've wasted it so
Help me Jesus I know what I am
Now that I know that I've need you so
Help me Jesus, my soul's in your hand.

Tell me Lord, if you think there's a way
I can try to repay
All I've taken from you
Maybe Lord, I can show someone else
What I've been through myself
On my way back to you.

Lord help me Jesus, I've wasted it so
Help me Jesus I know what I am
Now that I know that I've need you so
Help me Jesus, my soul's in your hand.

Paul's closing remarks to this section of the Philippian letter answers the "Why me, Lord?" question -- *"For it has been granted to you on behalf of Christ not only to believe on him, but also to suffer for him..."* Philippians 1:29.

This classic "come to Jesus" hit song was born out of struggle when a spiritually broken Kristofferson came to Jesus at a church meeting in the early 70's. Since then it has been sung by over a dozen recording artists (including Johnny Cash, Elvis Presley, and David Crowder) that realized how much their own attitude adjustment was dependent on the help that comes from Jesus and His presence in us.

In Colossians, we are challenged to: *"Let the word of Christ dwell in you richly as you teach and admonish one another with all wisdom, and as you* **sing psalms, hymns and spiritual songs with gratitude in your hearts to God.***"* (Colossians 3:16) Our attitude (our frame of mind) will adjust to truth as we learn to submit to it. Any and every mechanism to assist us in adjusting our attitude (whether a song, a book, the Scriptures, a friend, or our own mental discipline), can enable us to rise above suffering, struggles, problems and difficulties to enjoy Christ's presence when we need him the most.

BENEFITS OF A CHRIST-LIKE ATTITUDE

OPEN IN PRAYER. As a group practice some gratitude together. Remember that the key word for the Book of Philippians is "rejoice." There are 16 times where Paul reminds the reader that an attitude of gratitude is at the heart of a confident believer.

Attitude Check. Review the practice session from last week. Have everyone share their experience. Discuss this mixer question as a group or break into smaller numbers. Can you think of an example or two of someone (you included) who displayed a great attitude in a difficult situation and how it improved or accentuated other's awareness of Jesus (this could include Biblical examples as well)?

DIVING DEEPER

GROUP OBSERVATION

Read Philippians 1:12-30 and process the following questions together as a group:

1. How does Paul's attitude during his difficulties create benefits for spreading the gospel (God's good news)?

2. How does Paul's example to the Philippians in these verses match his exhortation to them in verse 27?

3. How do you think a person's attitude today might affect their surroundings like Paul's attitude affected his surroundings? Have you ever seen a contemporary example of someone who faced difficulties and trials in such a way that it:
   a. Advanced the gospel (the message of Christ's love) vs 12?
   b. Added clarity to the gospel (Christian message) vs 13?
   c. Inspired courage in others vs 14-26?

4. What does Paul tell himself about his struggles in vs 19-20?

Life Application: Earlier we learned that Paul's attitude (what he told himself about his circumstances) came from, or could be connected to:

His faith; trust that God would use the difficulties for His good (vs 19-20).
An eternal perspective; his ultimate security in being with Christ (vs 21-23).
An ability to see others' needs above his own (vs 24-26).

Share with one another how any of these, can be applied to a challenge you have faced, or are facing. Could any of these empower you to change your mind more quickly if you were mindful of them? For example, if someone wanted to borrow something of yours that you've never loaned out before, and at first you didn't want to let them use it, how might an eternal perspective, or considering others needs above your own, empower you to change your mind?

The last few verses of this chapter (27-30) bring two very important benefits to a Christ-like attitude. Evaluating the text and your life personally, can you see any effect on the unity we can have with others and our ability to endure difficulties when we face them together instead of alone? Please share your insight with the group.

PRACTICE THIS WEEK. Choose one or two things you will apply from today's study and report back next week about how you were able to implement the application.

SOAP ASSIGNMENT. Below are the Scriptures to SOAP this next week. If you have never done a SOAP exercise before, review the instructions located in the front of this Study Guide. During your small group time, consider having one or two people share their SOAP with the group, or pair-up and share with one other person.
- **Philippians 2:1-4**
- **Ephesians 4:2-6**
- **1 Peter 5:5-6**

Leaders:
Have members of your group break into groups of two or three and share what they will work to apply from this week's lesson. Encourage them to do the practice section before your next session. Close in prayer.

 **KIDS & ADULTS** Please engage your child, grandchild or mentee in a discussion around the following story/illustration. My wife Debbie, a Marriage and Family Therapist, was coaching our 4-year old granddaughter with a powerful skill that we often fail to employ even as adults. The skill to change your mind quickly.

After watching our granddaughter play with her dad's phone, navigating easily through multiple videos, changing her mind about one video and then another, Debbie encouraged her to see this ability as one she could also apply to the way she responds to the circumstances around her. She could quickly decide to have a good attitude instead of just winning. She could make the decision to share with her sister, in a moment's response, just as quickly and effectively as she decides and selects a different movie to watch.

What are some things that you change your mind about quickly, easily and effectively? Why do you think it's more difficult to change our mind when it comes to going from a bad attitude to a good one?

WEEK FOUR

THE ULTIMATE ATTITUDE

THIS WEEK'S THEME.

The ultimate attitude of humility.
This week we'll examine how humility is at the core
of what it takes to imitate Christ, follow his example,
and to demonstrate the unity he calls us to.

HOW WAS YOUR WEEK?

Remember Mad Libs? Fill in the blanks and you'll end up with a crazy story. Let's do some with your group. Pair up with someone, fill in the blanks, read it out loud and let the hilarity ensue.

Dear _____
  person in the room

I was writing to let you know that I hit your _____ while I was
                                                    noun

_____ to work. I backed out of the _____ and a(n)
verb ending in -ing   noun

_____ _____ ran across the _____ so I had
    adjective   animal   noun

to swerve to miss it. Sorry for hitting your _____. I hope you accept this
                                                    noun

_____ as a token of my sincere apology. Please do not be _____.
    noun   emotion

Sincerely,
your _____ neighbor.
        emotion

58

Take a few minutes to reflect on your week. Have you noticed a difference in your attitude since the start of this study?

_____

_____

_____

_____

_____

_____

_____

_____

_____

_____

_____

_____

_____

YOU ARE LOOKIN' GOOD!

Philippians 2:1-2 *"If you have any encouragement from being united with Christ, if any comfort from his love, if any fellowship with the Spirit, if any tenderness and compassion, then make my joy complete by being like-minded, having the same love, being one in spirit and of one mind."*

Fashion is a crazy thing. It is fascinating to me what some people will wear or what kinds of apparel will show up in pop culture. The Emmy's are always a fun thing to watch. I should clarify that. I actually never watch the Emmy's, but I have often watched the replays of the best and worst dressed at the Emmy's. It is interesting how some elements of fashion will find a resurgence after being completely dead.

I thought that bell-bottoms were dead, but apparently, they are not. I thought skinny pant legs were out, but wow, they not only came back, they're tighter and skinnier than ever. I ordered some skinny jeans not too long ago (actually the wife did - you know, trying to keep up with the times). Once I got into them I could hardly get out of them. I thought I might have to cut them off. After extracting myself, I sent them right back to the manufacturer. They were too skinny for me.

Every day you get up, take a gander through your closet and choose something to wear. Wait, that's actually not true for everyone. Some of you just throw on whatever is closest to the foot of your bed. But most of us, before we venture out into the public domain, give considerable deliberation to what we will put on. There are some of us who actually obsess over this selection process and find it to be extremely stressful. So much so that we throw up our arms in exasperation, screaming that we have nothing to wear, which is not exactly true. Most of us have plenty of things to wear, but with our frame of mind bent by our culture's obsession with how we look, clothing is a big deal.

By and large most of us make reasonable choices about what to wear, and look reasonably put together (except for a few of us who need serious help). The Biblical authors understood fashion. They knew so well "what not to wear" that they could have had their own fashion show. Read below what Peter and Paul say about fashion.

1 Peter 5:5b *"All of you, **clothe** yourselves with humility toward one another, because God opposes the proud but gives grace to the humble."*

Colossians 3:12 (Paul) *"Therefore, as God's chosen people, holy and dearly loved, **clothe** yourselves with compassion, kindness, humility, gentleness and patience."*

Like putting on our favorite shirt, shoes, or dress, we can also choose to put on our best attitude. Yep, all of the attitudinal traits listed in these passages are within our reach. They hang in our spiritual closets waiting to be put on. Fashion is a choice. Most of us have a style that we have chosen, to match with or help accentuate our physical identity. We think about, try on and put off things that we determine, just don't fit us well. They don't match our body shape, our taste, our work or our perceived social status.

We have to find our spiritual motivation. We are motivated all the time to look better on the outside. When we get serious about our spiritual identity (instead of just our physical identity), we begin to realize that we've been putting on some things that accentuate unflattering elements of who we have been. When we begin to cultivate who God calls us to be, it's like a spiritual makeover begins to take place right before our eyes.

A spiritual makeover is a choice. We learn to put off certain attitudes because we realize they just don't fit; they don't compliment us at all. The grouchy, impatient, condescending, stuck-up attitudes of the past not only need to be deselected, they need to be thrown out of our closet of choices.

The sooner we are aware of the best selections for our body shape and style, the sooner we are hearing friends and family affirming us with, "you are looking good!" That's even more true of your attitude. The sooner you can put off the acts (or attitudes) of your sinful nature, and put on the attitudes of the Spirit, the more attractive you will be.

UNNATURAL

Philippians 2:3-4 *"Do nothing out of selfish ambition or vain conceit, but in humility consider others better than yourselves. Each of you should look not only to your own interests but also the interests of others."*

Unnatural - that's what that sounds like. Did you ever watch a well-trained gymnast and simply be amazed at what they do and how natural they make it look? Almost all professional athletes do what they do and make it look easy; like they've been doing it their whole life. And, truth be known, most of them have.

Michael Phelps, the most decorated Olympic athlete in history, grew up in a family of competitive swimmers and began swimming when he was seven. Simone Biles started gymnastic in preschool and was competing by eight. Michael Jordan was playing basketball at an early age trying to catch up with his older brother's skills, and Tiger Woods was teeing off with his father at two. No one would say that any of the above athletes lacked talent, but what took that talent to the level of amazing was the love of the game, their sport, and the discipline and commitment to practice. The result being, that they make what is unnatural--*three back flips in a row, a single handed flying slam dunk, or a chip shot an inch from the hole*--look natural.

In Philippians 2:3-4, Paul challenges us to do something that goes against what is normal, and will never become natural until we have an increased love for Christ and others, and a commitment to practice the attitudinal skills necessary for healthy community. Setting aside our "selfish ambition"

> Exchanging our doubts for His faith, our despair for His hope, our sadness for His joy, our weakness for His strength.

and "vain conceit" is often the last thought in our minds - even on our good days. "Considering others better than ourselves" is not only unnatural, it's also unsustainable without a completely different expectation of how to achieve such a daunting task.

For this kind of shift to begin reshaping how we behave, Paul suggests we must be propelled by a new motivation -- *"If you have any encouragement from being united with Christ, and comfort from His love, any fellowship with the Spirit, any tenderness and compassion, then make my joy complete by being like-minded, having the same love, being one in spirit and purpose"* Philippians 2:1-2.

That is the 'love of the game'. It is what happens to a young athlete when they become fixed on a frame of mind that says - this is the most important thing for me to do. Paul is pulling out all the stops. He's saying, *For goodness' sake, if Jesus means anything to you - His love, acceptance, and forgiveness - if seeing others come together as one in that love does anything to your perspective, then let Christ infuse you with the passion to be like Him'* (Paraphrase, Philippians 2:1-2).

This whole passage pivots around Christ Jesus. Until being like Him becomes our *ultimate goal*, we will struggle to follow the *ultimate example* of Christ. A Christ-like attitude doesn't happen because we flip a switch, say a prayer, or go to church regularly. It happens when we rearrange the affairs of our life to submit to His will and follow His lead. That is the *ultimate motivation*; love for Christ that compels us to be like Him, to love like He loves, to care like

He cares, and set aside ourselves to put Him at the center of our thoughts, desires and decisions.

If we were to hear stories from the most exceptional athletes, there would be a familiar thread - someone, somewhere, saw them. They spoke into their story and said, "You could be really good at that - you have talent! Would you like me to coach you, come to my gym, try out for our team?" And they did, because someone saw them, believed in them, and called it out of them. They excelled. They stretched themselves and reached for the best that they could be. That's what Jesus wants to do in your life. He sees you, and knows that within you there is latent potential, talent, passion, desire and focus that is waiting to be called out and developed.

This is what attitude is all about - exchanging our doubts for His faith, our despair for His hope, our sadness for His joy, and our weakness for His strength. We are united with Christ. He alone has purchased us for himself and put us in right standing with God. As his beloved children, we have at our disposal every day, every hour, and every minute the comfort of His love. We never need to question that He is entirely, completely and passionately for us.

When we learn to daily disconnect ourselves from selfish ambition, and instead, fasten our minds to the supernatural reality of His presence, He begins to transform our attitudes. He moves us away from our suspicion that we are unlovely and unwanted. Our attention is redirected to what He has done to make us acceptable; His relentless commitment to finish what He has started within us - making us, thought by thought, more like Him.

He is empowering us to recognize our reactivity and sacrifice it; to put it to death and refuse to give

it life. By letting the reassurance of His presence, the fellowship of His Spirit and His tenderness and compassion energize our spirits, we can become like-minded, having the same love and being one in spirit and purpose. This kind of transformation-- or metamorphosis from unnatural to natural, from flesh to spirit, from willfulness to willingness-- happens when we step out of our *mindlessness* into a *mindfulness* of His presence.

When we make this our daily practice by refusing to let anything else interrupt our commitment to daily surrender all we are to Him, and invite His word and truth into our deepest place of meditation, we are no longer the same. Something that was once completely unnatural is now becoming our new normal.

THE ULTIMATE ATTITUDE

OPEN IN PRAYER. Continue to cultivate your gratitude by breaking into groups of 2 or 3 and practicing gratitude for something that was a challenge this past week (consider last week's theme of having a good attitude in tough times).

Attitude Check. Review the practice session from last week. Have everyone share their experience. Ask everyone in your group to to share a time when they were humiliated, have them break into pairs and share with just one other person. (If you can share first, a time that you were humiliated, that will help others to be vulnerable. It could be something that you can now, in retrospect, laugh at). Then ask, what is the correlation between humility and humiliation. What is the difference? How would a humble spirit/attitude potentially mitigate an experience of humiliation?

DIVING DEEPER

Option 1) Motivation
GROUP OBSERVATION

Ask everyone to quickly review Philippians 2:1-5 below. Ask if they can see any cause and effect in the passage. For example, is there any "because of this... then do this..." suggested in the text? How does this point to motivation? What is Paul saying to the Philippians about what should motivate them?

Philippians 2:1-5 *"Therefore if you have any encouragement from being united with Christ, if any comfort from his love, if any common sharing in the Spirit, if any tenderness and compassion, then make my joy complete by being like-minded, having the same love, being one in spirit and of one mind. Do nothing out of selfish ambition or vain conceit. Rather, in humility value others above yourselves, not looking to your own interests but each of you to the interests of the others. In your relationships with one another, have the same mindset as Christ Jesus."*

Leaders:
Depending on the remaining time you have, select one or more of the sections to process with your group.

Life Application: From day to day where do you find your motivation? How would you answer the "if" questions that Paul asks in Philippians 2:1? What does it mean to be united with Christ; to be comforted by His love and have fellowship with the Holy Spirit?

Earlier in our devotional reading for this week, we understood there is an "ultimate motivation." What is that motivation? Do you think you have any power to decide what your motivation is? If so, how do you do that?

Option 2) Demonstration
GROUP OBSERVATION

A. Read Philippians 2:2 below. What was the effect or action that Paul was trying to move the Philippians toward? Can you see the concept of unity in this passage?

Philippians 2:2 *"Then make my joy complete by being like minded, having the same love, being one in spirit and purpose."*

B. Read John 17:20b-21 and Ephesians 4:1-5 below and compare the ideas in each passage. How or why might this be an ultimate demonstration?

John 17:20b-21 *"I pray also for those who will believe in me through their message that all of them may be one Father just as you are in me and I am in you. May they also be in us, so that the world may believe that you have sent me."*

Ephesians 4:2-6 *"Be completely humble and gentle; be patient, bearing with one another in love. Make every effort to keep the unity of the Spirit through the bond of peace. There is one body and one Spirit, just as you were called to one hope when you were called; one Lord, one faith, one baptism; one God and Father of all, who is over all and through all and in all."*

Life Application: How are you implementing unity in your marriage, family, school, or church? What do the passages you just read say we have to do in order to have such unity?

Do the math: What does the following passage ask us to subtract and what are we to add or multiply? How have you, or how are you learning to live in a way that humility is cultivated?

Philippians 2:3-4 *"Do nothing out of selfish ambition or vain conceit, but in humility consider others better than yourselves. Each of you should look not only to your own interests but also the interests of others."*

Option 3) Inspiration
GROUP OBSERVATION

In Philippians 2:5-12, we see Jesus lifted up as the ultimate example. Take a moment and read this passage together as a group. What strikes you most about this passage? How does what Jesus did, serve as an example for us, in what Paul has asked us to do in previous verses?

Life Application: How does inspiration empower you to be more engaged? What are some ways you can tap into Jesus for greater inspiration than you do currently? If humility is the ultimate attitude, what would that look like in your life and relationships?

Leaders:
Review the Practice This Week with your group. Ask someone in your group to close your time in prayer. Ask them to pray specifically for all of us to grow in our ability to live in humility with one another.

PRACTICE THIS WEEK. Choose one or two things you will apply from today's study and report back next week about how you were able to implement the application.

SOAP ASSIGNMENT. Below are the Scriptures to SOAP this next week. If you have never done a SOAP exercise before, review the instructions located in the front of this Study Guide. During your small group time, consider having one or two people share their SOAP with the group, or pair-up and share with one other person.
- **Philippians 2:12-13**
- **Philippians 2:14-18**

KIDS & ADULTS

Help your youth understand the power of choice when it comes to an attitude of humility. Ask them, "why did you choose to wear the clothes you have on today?" See if there was any choice that they can detect, or if it was just the easiest choice—less wrinkled, clean, on the floor, closest to the bed, etc. How does the day's activities influence their choice of what to wear?

Next, ask what they think it means to be humble—what does being humble look like? Sometimes it is easier to understand a concept when it is examined from the opposite perspective. Therefore, tease out the concept of humility by asking what pride looks like. Do they think these concepts are good or bad, if so, why?

Read 1 Peter 5:5b-6 together and process the following questions, *"All of you, clothe yourselves with humility toward one another, because God opposes the proud but gives grace to the humble. Humble yourselves, therefore, under God's mighty hand, that He may lift you up in due time."*

• What do they think this passage is saying about both pride and humility. Since they clothe themselves every day, what does that say about clothing oneself in humility?

• Ask how they think humility is "put on." Help them to see that just as they choose what to wear, they can choose their attitude. Have fun - don't be too serious! Seek to make learning an ongoing conversation around what we believe and tell ourselves about our choices.

Leaders:
Remember to use the Kids & Adults section as a way to encourage everyone to see themselves (parents, grandparents, and mentors) as spiritual influencers of the youth around them. If we fail to have spiritual conversations with the youth around us, there will remain an unhealthy separation from day-to-day life and spiritual choices. Conversely, the more we engage in spiritual conversations the

WEEK FIVE

HOW TO BUILD A BETTER ATTITUDE

THIS WEEK'S THEME.

Building a Better Attitude.

This week we'll examine how to build a better attitude. The key verse in this week's focus is Philippians 2:12 *"Therefore my dear friends, as you have always obeyed, not only in my presence, but now much more in my absence- continue to work out your salvation..."* To have a better attitude, it is helpful to work a plan to actually change our attitude. In this week's material, there are three keys suggested for working a plan to have a better attitude.

HOW WAS YOUR WEEK?

Draw your most prevalent attitude from this past week. Don't be afraid to add some color!

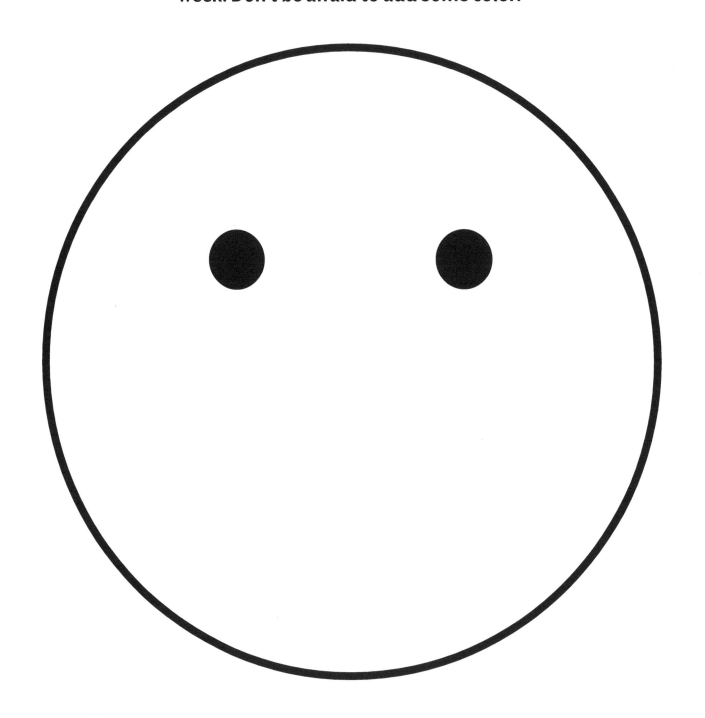

Take a few minutes to write about your attitudes this week. Were they positive or were they negative?

_____

_____

_____

_____

_____

_____

_____

_____

_____

_____

_____

_____

WHAT IF "IT" HAPPENS

Philippians 2:12 *"Therefore, my dear friends, as you have always obeyed--not only in my presence, but now much more in my absence--continue to work out your salvation with fear and trembling."*

You can't work out what you are not working in. The challenge in Philippians 2:12 is a call to action, planning and follow through. When we are truly working out what God is working in, we find ourselves more prepared for whatever lies ahead. Without such preparedness we are more inclined to struggle with, and be distracted by even little things.

Have you ever been asked by someone during a time of difficulty, "how are you handling that?" A parent is ill, a boyfriend is unfaithful, a job ends or an illness is detected. Things happen, right? But how we deal with the unexpected does not have to be "unexpected." Most people would say about someone else's crisis, "I don't know how I would handle that if it were to happen to me." But to one degree or another "it" will happen to you. Maybe you'll never be the victim of a school or work shooting, let's hope not. Maybe no one will ever break into your house or car. Maybe no one in your family will ever get cancer, or be fired or have an affair. But for many reading this, they are already saying to themselves, "Yeah, that's what I thought" because the "It" has happened to them.

In our day and age we have all kinds of preparedness training. Some analytical, proactive over-thinker is putting together a plan for what to do when someone does what no one thought someone would do. So now, we have plans and agendas for "active shooter training, terrorist threat training, bomb threat procedures, evacuation plans and fightback training." It goes on and on, and rightfully so.

Martin Luther King Jr. said it like this, *"When evil men plot, good men must plan. When evil men burn and bomb, good men must build and bind. When evil men shout ugly words of hatred, good men must commit themselves to the glories of love."*

Wow, that could have been written this week and we'd all say, "yes," that's what this season in history needs. It's what was needed fifty years ago, a hundred years ago and three weeks ago. Until Jesus comes back that's what every season in history needs.

Much of what is at the heart of any proactive awareness and training is the need for someone to have a cool head when others are hot; a calm approach when other are running wild. Someone has to step out of the panic zone into the plan. Without a plan, that's pretty hard to do.

The need for a calm attitude squarely lands on those wanting to be a part of the solution instead of just frantically trying to escape the problem.

The good news is, that in a world where STUFF happens, we can be engaged in attitude awareness training. It's not just for the first responder, but for all of us so we can better respond to whatever crisis we find ourselves up against.

I remember hearing Dr. Cronk, one of the scholars who did the translation work on the NIV Bible, say at a lecture I attended, "The way you handle your little problems will determine how you handle your big problems." If we don't begin to develop preparedness for little crises, we won't be prepared for the big crises that are inevitably going to happen somewhere close to us, if not to us. The greater my ability to arrest a poor attitude during the disappointments of life, the greater I'll be at arresting and altering my attitude during the disasters in life.

When we take responsibility to work out our salvation—to be engaged in the process of spiritual transformation—we are preparing ourselves for whatever God wants to do next on our journey with Him.

Simply asking God to help you have an attitude that is prepared for a challenge is the starting point. Then seeking out mentors that can give you direction and feedback is critical. The more you work this kind of conversation into the fabric of your life and relationships, the more it becomes second nature. And when a crisis hits, you'll be more prepared.

LOVE-BASED OBEDIENCE

I love being a grandfather, I have the most adorable grandchildren. They are adorable not because they are compliant, obedient, or always well-behaved, but because they are mine. They are my baby girl's girls (we have boy and a grandchild on the way). I will often hold them close and whisper in their ear, "I love you...grandpa loves you."

They are good girls, naturally a bit mischievous, independent, and precocious. They have a built-in proclivity to comply with authority, while that authority is squarely in front of them. But the moment that authority (be it mom, dad, grandma or grandpa) has turned away, their compliance goes out the window. The cupcake they were instructed not to touch, has now been pierced by a little finger. The toy that their "sister had first" is now being snatched away, or the dog they were told to be gentle with is now being ridden like rodeo bull.

This is all understandable when we are under five, but 25, 35, or 45... what's our excuse? Ok - am I hitting close to home or do I need to get more specific? What do you do when no one is looking? Can you identify and own up to any drift in your behavior that takes place when there is no one around that puts your behavior in check? I'm not saying that your spouse, roommate or parent is keeping watch over your choices. They probably are not. But when they have left the building, do you ever watch something that would have been better unwatched? Do you turn to a bottle of alcohol, or a drug that you want to remain

hidden? Do you ever eat something or increase your volume of food consumption because no one is around? Do you text someone that is on your vulnerable list - people best not communicated with? Do you enter into a conversation with someone that crosses a line when there's no one present that would challenge your choice?

Somewhere, sometime, to some degree, I'd wager that we've all had some drift in our choices; we drift away from "doing the right thing." I love how the apostle Paul compliments the Philippian believers in Philippians 2:12 *"...my dear friends, **as you have always obeyed--not only in my presence, but now much more in my absence--** continue to work out your salvation with fear and trembling..."*

Listen carefully, He is whispering, "I love you."

This is an outstanding shift (I call that love-based obedience) that conquers the drift that can often occur when no one is present. They (the Philippian believers) were obeying not just in Paul's presence, but also in his absence. The word used here for obey is the Greek word *Hupakouo.* I love this word. It is a compound word. Hupo=*under*, and akouo=*to listen* or *consider what is said.* It is where we get our word acoustics.

There are two splendid things about this word. First, it was used in secular Greek for a doorman; someone who attended a door and listened for the voice of one who wished to enter the room where they were serving. When we have love-based obedience, we are constantly listening for the Lord's voice. And when we hear Him, we quickly open the door of obedience so we can enter into His purpose.

When we are hard of hearing (spiritually speaking), or still have an underdeveloped obedience (like that of a child) we tend to close the door to God's best. Spiritual growth, development and maturity is marked by an obedience when no one else is present. Because it is not their voice that matters or motivates us, but His.

Secondly, when we are in a room or space that has good acoustics, we can hear without the need for artificial amplification. When we have developed our love-based obedience, we have improved our spiritual acoustics. Something I learned from Dr. Henry Cloud—an acclaimed leadership expert, psychologist, and best-selling author of the book, *Boundaries*—is that when you are struggling to do what you know needs to happen; when you are likely to acquiesce to indifference or disobedience, apply external structure. This isn't the long-term goal, but if your spiritual acoustics are not good, or underdeveloped, then you need amplification. You need structure. For the alcoholic that is barely out of denial, structure is critical. You don't go into a bar saying you're only going to eat the peanuts. If you are made of dynamite you don't stoke fires.

I love my grandbabies! I don't love them less because they haven't grown past the need for structure - I continue to be a part of the network of loving adults who provide the structure that they need knowing their love will mature. How are your spiritual acoustics? Are you learning to open the door to His voice? The speed of your ability to adjust your attitude will be in direct proportion to your spiritual acoustics. Listen carefully, He is whispering, *"I love you."*

MEMORY
VERSE

Philippians 2:3-5
"Do nothing out of selfish ambition or vain conceit, but in humility consider others better than yourselves. Each of you should look not only to your own interests, but also to the interests of others. Your attitude should be the same as that of Christ Jesus."

HOW TO BUILD A BETTER ATTITUDE

OPEN IN PRAYER. Continue to cultivate your gratitude by breaking into groups of 2 or 3, and practicing gratitude for something about Christ's example described in last week's material, and then pray for each other.

Attitude Check. Review the practice session from last week. Have everyone share their experience. Choose one of the following two options for discussion:

1. Share a time when you were disobedient; when you were with an authority figure and then in their absence, were disobedient. What did that say about the integrity or maturity of your commitment?

2. Share how having a personal example to follow (someone who modeled some better behavior) made all the difference in improving some aspect of your life.

DIVING DEEPER

Option 1) A Better Example
GROUP OBSERVATION

Do you remember what a "therefore" is there for? How, or why, do you think Paul is wanting to follow up on what he has told us about Jesus as the ultimate example in Philippians 2:5-11?

Leaders:
Select one or more of the Diving Deeper options to process with your group.

Review the following passages. How important is it to Paul that we recognize our need for good examples? How is Jesus the better example?

Philippians 3:17 *"Join with others in following my example..."*

Philippians 4:9a *"Whatever you have learned or received or heard from me, or seen in me-put it into practice..."*

Life Application: How can you practically utilize Jesus as your best example? Share some things that you have done or that you think could be done to better follow Jesus? Who are some of your human examples that you draw upon for insight and modeling Christ-like behavior? What have you seen in them that you try to imitate?

Option 2) A Better Obedience
GROUP OBSERVATION

How are the following verses similar and what is the message we can draw from them?

Philippians 2:12 *"Therefore as you have always obeyed, not only in my presence, but now much more in my absence, continue to work out your salvation with fear and trembling..."*

Philippians 1:27 *"Whatever happens, conduct yourselves in a manner worthy of the gospel of Christ. Then, whether I come and see you, or only hear about you in my absence, I will know that you stand firm in one Spirit, contending as one man for the faith of the gospel."*

The word "obey" is Hupakouo in the Greek: Hupa=under; Kouo=hear. It means, literally, "to hear under". It is from this word "Kouo" that we get our word acoustics. What are acoustics and what difference do "good acoustics" make in a building or auditorium to an audience? What do these passages suggest make good spiritual acoustics?

Life Application: What can you do to improve your spiritual acoustics? How might unity and community help someone to acquire a better obedience?

Option 3) A Better Awareness
GROUP OBSERVATION

As a group discuss the following three results of a better awareness.

   1. A better awareness actively participates in salvation.

Philippians 2:12-b-13 *"... work out your salvation with fear and trembling, for it is God who works in you to will and to act according to his good purpose."*

2. A better awareness can recognize and eliminate attitude killers.

Philippians 2:14 *"Do everything without complaining and arguing..."*

3. A better awareness embraces a new identity that reflects the light of Christ.

Philippians 2:15-18 *"...so that you may become blameless and pure, children of God without fault in a crooked and depraved generation, in which you shine like stars in the universe as you hold out the word of life. But even if I am being poured out like a drink offering on the sacrifice and service coming from your faith, I am glad and rejoice with all of you. So you too should be glad and rejoice with me."*

Life Application: Looking over the above observation about a better awareness, process the following questions with your group:

1. How would you describe your part of working out your salvation? The Bible clearly tells us that we cannot save ourselves, so what is our part?

2. How does complaining and arguing affect attitude? How could a better awareness empower you to recognize and eliminate attitude killers?

3. What difference does a perspective of being "children of God...shining like stars in the universe...holding out the word of life..." have on attitude?

Leaders:
Review the Practice This Week with your group. Either have someone close in prayer or pair-up and pray for each other. Ask God to light something up from this week's material that you will want to focus on to build a better attitude.

PRACTICE THIS WEEK. Choose one or two things you will apply from today's study and report back next week about how you were able to implement the application.

SOAP ASSIGNMENT. Below are the Scriptures to SOAP this next week. If you have never done a SOAP exercise before, review the instructions located in the front of this Study Guide. During your small group time, consider having one or two people share their SOAP with the group, or pair-up and share with one other person.

- **Philippians 4:9**
- **Philippians 2:25-30**
- **Philippians 2:19-24**

KIDS & ADULTS

Using similar questions as the "Attitude Check", help your youth to begin thinking about each of these concepts: (1) obedience when no adult is present and (2) identifying a better example to follow. Create an accepting environment for them to share honestly and resist any temptation to become corrective or lecture. Also, let them talk, and listen to their feelings and ideas without judgment. It will be powerful for them to share openly if they struggle to comply with standards of behavior when alone or away from authority figures. Actually bringing this reality (most of us, to some degree, have struggled in this area) to the surface in an accepting context can empower change.

Question #1: *"Why do you think there is a struggle to 'do the right thing' when alone or away from a parent/adult leader?"* This could create a healthy discussion around the reality of our "flesh/sinful nature" or around the desire to be accepted by others (peer-pressure). They may also share about their curiosity around some "off-limit substance" that could influence their struggle to obey when they are alone, or no adult/parent is around.

Question #2: The second question is less tricky but equally valuable. *"Who do you believe are the best examples that you have in your life to follow?"* Don't react if you are not on their list. Just affirm their response and let them think out loud about what might make a good example. Ask the following questions, "How is Jesus a better example? What do you think Jesus did that we should try and follow?"

Leaders:
Remember to use the Kids & Adults section as a way to encourage everyone to see themselves (parents, grandparents and mentors) as spiritual influencers of the youth around them. The questions can be spread over several days or conversations. Don't feel like you have to start and finish the conversation in one setting. It may be more powerful if it is spread over several days. This is a powerful way to help our youth engage in thinking and processing honestly about life and choices.

WEEK SIX

MORE MALE MODELS

THIS WEEK'S THEME.
Being a good model or mentor to others means we have had a good model or mentor.

HOW WAS YOUR WEEK?

We all wear different masks. Some are more decorative than others, depending on our own personality and/or who we are with. Color, draw, or craft this mask to represent a mask you may wear sometimes.
Feel free to cut it out and wear it in your small group.

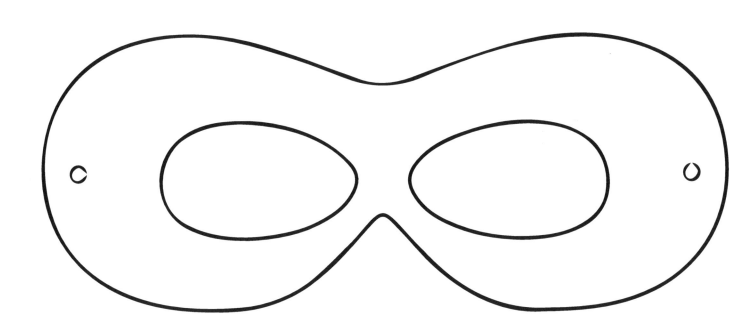

What's a "mask" you've worn before?

_____

_____

_____

_____

_____

_____

_____

_____

_____

_____

_____

_____

_____

NOT JUST A PRETTY FACE

It is not hard to find a pretty face. Have you ever been distracted at the grocery checkout counter by all of the periodicals? Man, there are more beautiful people out there than you can shake a stick at. It can be either super discouraging because we can feel like we'll never look like them, or super motivational--if we could just get the right teeth whitener, skin cream, or a tummy tuck.

I have heard people say of a good-looking guy, "he's so handsome, he could be a model!" You know... someone who is paid to just stand there and look good, or maybe in some cases, to refine and hone their ability to do "the walk" -- as in walk down the runway. That takes some real talent. You have to stay upright and sway from one side to the other--to just the right degree. You've got to be super careful to not fall on your face. I mean that's tough stuff! I am not saying that models aren't talented, I just think their talent is usually covered up by their looks.

For the most part, (of course you can disagree with me), male models got what they've got from their mommas and the good Lord. They didn't choose to have high cheekbones, a chiseled chin, broad shoulders and a thick head of hair - right? Isn't that what they say, "If you've got it, you've got it." Shake what your momma gave you!

Let me tell you what is hard. It's hard to find character that is deep. Someone once said that, "beauty is only skin deep, but ugly goes clear to the bone". That's what character does. It's not skin deep, it goes clear to the bone. If you want to find men and women of deep character it's going to take a heck of a lot more than showing up at a photoshoot. True character, integrity, values and faithfulness are not things we are born with. They must be cultivated, and they are the byproduct, not of an easy life, but usually of a life refined by trials, hardship and discipline.

God knows I wish it were easy. I would love to have been born with character (it would have been nice to have the looks too), but it's not what you've been born with, it is what's been born out of life's challenges that makes us who we are. In the middle of the little book of Philippians, the apostle Paul writes a reference letter for two male models. Not the kind that shock you with their looks, but the kind that shock you with how they've looked to Jesus throughout life's trials. Timothy and Epaphroditus are well known names in the New Testament - not because they were "super apostles" or one of the twelve, but because they were entrusted with a plan and invited into an apprenticeship that they stuck with.

Each of these men were blessed with a mentor. Paul, himself, poured into them, which elevated them to the status of being models; men worthy of emulation and adoration. In Philippians 2:29, Paul says about Epaphroditus, *"honor men like him."* And earlier in Philippians 2:19-20, 22, he says of Timothy, *"I have no one else like him, who takes a genuine interest in your welfare. For everyone looks out for his own interests, not those of Jesus Christ."* This is exactly what he has admonished all of us to be in Philippians 2:3 *"...value others above yourselves, not looking to your own interests but each of you to the interests of the others."*

Character, integrity, and humility come out of models that have learned to set aside their own interests for those of Christ and others. I am sure there are some godly fashion models out there somewhere, but what we need the most are everyday men and women who are modeling the kind of attitude and behavior that inspire us to say, *I want to look to Jesus and be more like him; to be an example of faithfulness when others are faithless; to be trustworthy when others are untrusted; and to have an attitude that builds up instead of one that tears down.*

You have been called by God to be a model. An example of compassion, kindness, humility and patience. The best way to be a great model is to have a great model. Who, besides Jesus are you learning from, and who are you seeking to be a model for?

THE MASKED MAN

Most of us can tell when someone's attitude is up or down, unless they are masters at hiding, or adjusting their attitude on the fly. They can look the same, but are actually completely different.

I walked into the room and could tell immediately that his spirit was down; his normal jovial personality was sullen, muted and distant.

"Steve, is something wrong, you don't seem to be yourself?" I asked.

"Not feeling it today Pastor." He replied.

"Not feeling it?" I reflected back. "What does that mean?"

Avoiding eye contact, he replied, "I just don't feel like I can put on the happy face and make myself look OK."

"Do you want to tell me what's going on?" I asked.

Steve went on to describe how things at home were not good. His wife moved out of the house and in with a friend, and was threatening to leave for good if Steve didn't face up to his drinking and get some help. I had suspected that he might have a drinking problem. I'd seen him put down several drinks in social settings and was a bit concerned myself. It seemed like one or two were never enough.

Steve always looked good and filled the room with a presence. If he was in attendance, everyone knew

"Being confident of this, that He who began a good work in you will carry it on to completion until the day of Christ Jesus."
Philippians 1:6

it and enjoyed his uplifting personality. This wasn't the first time his marriage had been shaken over this issue, but it was the first time Jean, his wife, had made such a bold move.

The emotional plunge that I was witnessing in Steve was real and warranted. The difference this time was that the normal coping and disguising Steve was so good at, wasn't able to push off the reality that when he went home that night, Jean wouldn't be there.

Being equipped to have a healthy attitude isn't about distorting or ignoring reality, but knowing how to face difficult things with the confidence of what God wants to accomplish.

When we are used to coping with life challenges the way Steve was, we learn to put on masks that seek to disguise our true assessment and perspective. Even when we can do this well, causing everyone around us to perceive we are fine, under the surface we know that deep down we are just pretending.

Apprehending a Christ-like attitude is not acting like we have one because we want others to think more highly of us. The attitude of Christ is one that is present, both when we are with people, and in complete isolation. It's not generated by the presence of others, but by our confidence in the presence and promises of Christ.

Over the next 6-12 months, my friend Steve joined a few of us who meet regularly to exercise and practice focusing on Jesus. He joined a recovery ministry that gave him a new place to live mask free. Little by little, I watched him learn to meditate on Scripture, live in community, and regularly confess and confront the compulsions that would, in the past, drive him to drink. He moved from being a masked man to one that was genuine, humble and sober.

The good work that God is committed to do in us, finds its greatest momentum when we learn that our state-of-mind (that which builds up or breaks down our attitude) is being cultivated every day by a growing awareness of who He is making us to be; and removing the masks, we may have been wearing most of our lives. Under every mask lies an authentic person longing to be free.

OPEN IN PRAYER. After opening in prayer, pair up and share with each other what you tried to apply or practice this past week from the previous weeks' material.

Attitude Check. Review the practice session from last week and share your experience with the group. Take out a pen and paper and privately write down the name of someone you know that resembles each of the following character traits. Do this one at a time together as a group, but only discuss those individuals associated with the positive traits: 1) Compassionate, 2) Critical, 3) Cooperative, 4) Competitive, 5) Committed, 6) Flaky, 7) Courageous, 8) Cowardly.

Ask yourself what you want to be known for; what character traits do you hope others will think of when they think of you?

DIVING DEEPER

Option 1) Compassion

GROUP OBSERVATION

Have someone read Philippians 2:19-30. How do you see compassion in either Timothy or Epaphroditus? What does the story of the "good Samaritan" tell us about compassion? Who else in history has served as an example of compassion?

Life Application: How have experiences of suffering or struggle impacted your ability to show compassion. Does anyone have an example of something they have gone through that increased their compassion toward others?

Leaders:
Select one or more of the Diving Deeper options to process with your group.

Option 2) Cooperation
GROUP OBSERVATION

In Philippians 2:22, Paul uses a metaphor to describe his mentoring relationship with Timothy. What is it? Now as a group, compare and contrast the words competition and cooperation. How are they different? Do you see competition as a good trait or a risky one, and why?

Philippians 2:22 *"Timothy has proved himself, because as a son with his father he has served with me in the work of the gospel."*

Life Application: Have you ever had a competitive relationship with someone that turned negative, and why? How have you seen cooperation benefit a family, business, friendship or church?

Option 3) Commitment and Courage
GROUP OBSERVATION

In the passage below, how does Paul's description of Epaphroditus illustrate commitment and courage?

Philippians 2:25-30 *"...Epaphroditus, my brother, fellow worker and fellow soldier, who is also your messenger, whom you sent to take care of my needs. ...Welcome him in the Lord with great joy, and honor men like him, because he almost died for the work of Christ, risking his life to make up for the help you could not give me."*

"my brother"
"fellow worker"
"fellow soldier"
"your messenger"
"risking his life"

Life Application: What would need to happen in our lives to get to this level of commitment or courage? What would fuel such solidarity? Do you think you would ever risk your life for strengthening or delivering the cause (message) of Christ, why or why not?

Option 4) Character
GROUP OBSERVATION

Both Timothy and Epaphroditus were mentored by Paul. How do you think mentoring fits into the growing of our character? What does Paul's statement about following his example tell us regarding the need to have a mentor in order to be a mentor?

Philippians 4:9 *"Whatever you have learned or received or heard from me, or seen in me--put it into practice. And the God of peace will be with you."*

Life Application: How does our "mentoring statement" challenge you toward this church-wide objective that we have to "Mentor the Next Generation"?

I Am A Mentor
"I will seek to be an example that anyone can follow; an observational mentor to all the youth in my sphere of influence and an intentional mentor to a few. I will memorize and meditate on Deuteronomy 6:6-9 and Philippians 4:9 to help me stay focused on this goal."

Where do you see your development in this statement/goal?
Have you decided that you want to be a good example?
Are you aware of the youth in your sphere of influence?
Have you identified any specific youth that you are intentionallly mentoring?
What would keep you from embracing such a commitment?

PRACTICE THIS WEEK. Choose one or two things you will apply from today's study and report back next week about how you were able to implement the application.

Leaders:
Review the Practice This Week with your group. Ask someone to close your time in prayer.

SOAP ASSIGNMENT. Below are the Scriptures to SOAP this next week. If you have never done a SOAP exercise before, review the instructions located in the front of this Study Guide. During your small group time, consider having one or two people share their SOAP with the group, or pair-up and share with one other person.
  · Philippians 4:4-7
   · James 1:2-4
    · Philippians 3:7-9

KIDS & ADULTS Help your youth understand the power of being a good example or model of some good behavior. Use the idea in the Additude Check to see who comes to their mind when they think of the character traits provided. Feel free to make up some of your own too, like "who makes you laugh?" or "who is good at being really kind or patient?" Ask them if they want to be known for some character quality. If so, which one?

This would be a great time to have some spontaneous prayer with your student. Spend a few minutes expressing some gratitude for the people in your life and theirs who are models of good behavior and good attitudes.

Leaders:
Use the Kids & Adults section to get feed back on who is using the questions with their kids, grandkids, or mentees? How is that going? What kind of conversations are happening?

WEEK SEVEN

HOW TO GUARD YOUR ATTITUDE

THIS WEEK'S THEME.

How to maintain an "attitude of gratitude."

HOW WAS YOUR WEEK?

Think about how your week went. Did you have a more righteous and Christ-like attitude or did you have a more negative attitude that ate you up?

If you had a positive attitude connect the numbers but if you had a negative attitude connect the letters.

Then take some time to reflect on your attitude below.

◆ ◆ ◆ ◆ ◆

_____

_____

_____

_____

_____

_____

_____

_____

_____

_____

_____

_____

_____

•2　　　•A　　　　　•22
　　　　　　　•Z
　　　　　　　•1
　　　　　　　•23
•3
　　•4
　　　　•Y　　　　　•B
　　　　　　•20
　　　　　•56　　•57 •24　　•25
•5　　　　　　　　　　　　　　•19
　　•X　•55　　　　　　•C
　　　　　　　　　　　•26
　　•54　•50　　　　•30
•W　　　　　　　　•D
•7　•49　•51　　•29　•31
•6　　•53　　　•28　•27　•17
　　•52　　　　　　•18
　　　•N　　•L
　•48
•V　•42　•43
　•P　•41　•44　•J　•E
　　　•M　•32
　•47　•40
•8　•O　•K　•16
　•46　•45　•33
•U　•37　•39　•38
　•36　•R　•F
•10　　•34　•14
　　•35
•9　　　•15 •I
　•11　　•13　•G
•Q　　　•T
•S •H
　•12

THE SPACE IN BETWEEN

Viktor Frankl *"Between stimulus and response there is a space. In that space is our power to choose our response. In our response lies our growth and our freedom."*

Would you consider yourself a reactive person? Is your response to some "stimulus" more negative than you would like? When your feathers are ruffled or someone pushes your buttons, how do you react? How about when someone pulls out in front of you, or is going super slow, or didn't use their blinker and is weaving through traffic? I can hear you now... 'It's not fair to use driving examples - we're all reactive to stupid drivers!' Yeah, maybe we are all tempted to be reactive to bad driving, but we are not all reactive to it.

> "Not everything faced can be changed, but nothing can be changed until it is faced."

You may ask, "what is being reactive?'" That's a good question. It is so common to be reactive, that we as a culture have collected dozens of descriptions to aid us in our logical displacement of taking any responsibility. So we defend ourselves by saying, "I'm not reactive! Occasionally, I may--jump to conclusions, get hot behind the collar, become a little defensive, snap at others, bite someone's head off, jump down their throat or carry a chip on my shoulder--but I'm not reactive. And if I am, well, of course anyone would be. After all, if they hadn't ruffled my feathers, pushed my buttons, got in my face, been so rude, treated me poorly, talked to me like that, or looked at me wrong, then it would be fine and I wouldn't have had to react that way."

Stimulus and response and the space in between has everything to do with attitude. Getting a handle on this whole concept isn't easy. Lord knows there is a ton of stimuli out there that can take us on a wild emotional ride. I used to be so reactive that I not only would have a flood of emotions hit me in the middle of a meeting, or conversations that I interpreted negatively (stimulus) and feel the need to defend myself in that moment (response), but would then feed the reactivity for hours, if not days. The only thing worse than having an unhealthy negative response to a bad situation, is continuing to have a negative response long after the stimulus has passed.

Many of us live in an emotional battle zone with ourselves. We fight the urge to react (negatively) to something said or done, and then, regardless of our overt response, we are plagued with emotional shrapnel for days - potentially never recovering from the negative mental conclusions, but rather adding them to the relational baggage we've learned to collect.

If you are anything like me, and you've experienced the weight of an unpleasant conversation, or better defined, an interpretation of an unpleasant conversation, then you know just how difficult it is to arrest our emotional reactivity at any given moment. Surely there's some criteria, or set of rules, that give us at least a little wiggle room for some "justifiable" reactivity - isn't there? For instance, isn't some measure of reactivity justified if a person says something offensive, or stupid, or rude, or they get too personal, or bring up politics or religion, or talk about your momma?

A bad attitude is never someone else's fault. They are not our nemesis. What we tell ourselves (in the space in between) is our nemesis. At some point we have to decide that we might just be a part (a big part) of the problem.

We can never change a problem we are unwilling to face. One of my mentors used to say, "Not everything faced can be changed, but nothing can be changed until it is faced." To successfully garner the emotional health and wellness that we crave, we have to get our arms around just how rapid our unconscious flood of mental messages, instinctively, take over our frame of mind.

Until we can confront the notion that we are helpless, we will remain helpless. But when we realize that we are capable of capturing this space between stimulus and response, we will begin to see a steady increase in our personal awareness and skill. This process takes time, self awareness, and a commitment to grow in our ability to capture the reactive messages firing in our heads that instigate or fuel the negative response we desire to overcome.

What we do with the "space in between" begins by recognizing there is a space, and instead of being victimized by it, we can become a victor over it. Instead of it controlling us, we can control it. The power of Christ's presence in us is described as *"the mind of Christ"* in 1 Corinthians 2:15-16. Because of this new power, we are no longer victims, or subject to our human interpretations. We now have Divine help to conquer what goes on between stimulus and response. And within that space, lies either our growth and freedom, or our bondage and captivity.

PROFIT & LOSS STATEMENT

Philippians 3:7-8 *"But whatever was to my profit I now consider loss for the sake of Christ. What is more, I consider everything a loss compared to the surpassing greatness of knowing Christ Jesus my Lord..."*

A Profit and Loss (P&L) statement is simply a document that communicates whether a business is profitable. It is about moving forward, not backward; making money, not losing money. It's the way a business assesses how it is doing and gains objectivity on its financial health. In Philippians 3:7-11, the apostle Paul gives a spiritual P&L. In a world that builds its identity on weaker things, it is easy to lose spiritual objectivity.

All of us want to be profitable. We want to do the kinds of things that move us forward and not backward. We desire profitable interaction with others and profitable financial choices, as well as good leadership, emotional and relational choices. John Maxwell speaks about a principle of leadership that he calls the Law of Respect. He points out that when you make good leadership decisions, it puts change in your pocket. When you make bad leadership decisions, it takes change out of your pocket. When you are out of change, you are out as a leader.

When we are good at business, the business grows in its profitability - making more money than it's losing. If we are good at relationships, our relationships are getting better, not worse. Most of us do regular P&Ls unconsciously and emotionally. We take an emotional assessment of ourselves and either feel good about where we are, or not. When our emotional P&L is low, our attitude will conversely be low. Just like a struggling business loses confidence from making poor business choices, so we also tend to lose confidence when our relational, social, and life choices are poor.

I believe when we are feeling good about ourselves, it's normally connected to the quality of our choices, which produce a greater sense of stability that bolsters our identity (how we see ourselves). As we take an emotional P&L, it is natural for us to feel better about ourselves when things are going well, because we see and believe those profits (relational, social, or financial) define us. They tell a story about who we are, and if we like that story, we feel better about ourselves. It's where we find our confidence.

No wonder so many successful people (in business) have an air of confidence. Their identity is bigger, stronger and seemingly more stable because of their personal achievements. The better the achievement, the better the identity. Paul provides us with a powerful juxtaposition or paradox in Philippians 3:7-11. He tells us that whatever was to his profit (and he gives a most impressive list), he now considers loss compared to the surpassing greatness of knowing Christ Jesus, His Lord.

Here's the big point. Where you find your confidence will typically be where you find your attitude. At any given moment, if you feel good about your relationships, it can boost your attitude (frame of mind). If you are feeling good about your finances, you experience a boost in your attitude about life and your financial stability.

This makes perfect sense, but it also creates a perfect problem. You are now a slave to whatever you deem boosts your identity - your looks, finances, relationships, whatever. Paul is wanting to assist us in a major paradigm shift that says, my attitude, my frame of mind, my identity is no longer based on whatever was to my profit, but is now based on my relationship and identity as a child of God and the surpassing greatness of knowing Christ Jesus, my Lord.

Until our spiritual assessment (our spiritual P&L) supersedes all other assessments, we will find our attitude is being moved by the winds of financial, emotional or relational changes instead of remaining secure in the One who promises to never change, but to be the same, yesterday, today and forever. Creating better spiritual objectivity is about becoming more aware of where you put your confidence (and find your identity) and then daily shifting that to your relationship with Christ. Today, let Jesus boost how you see yourself. Let Him redefine what matters most, and you will find your confidence in your relationship with Him.

Philippians 4:4-7
"Rejoice in the Lord always. I will say it again: Rejoice! Let your gentleness be evident to all. The Lord is near. Do not be anxious about anything, but in everything, by prayer and petition, with thanksgiving, present your requests to God. And the peace of God, which transcends all understanding, will guard your hearts and your minds in Christ Jesus."

HOW TO GUARD YOUR ATTITUDE

OPEN IN PRAYER. Ask someone to open your group time in prayer.

Attitude Check. Review the practice session from last week. Have everyone share their experience. A couple of quotes that we have heard during our Attitude series from Viktor Frankl include: (1) *Between stimulus and response there is a space. In that space is our power to choose our response. In our response lies our growth and our freedom*; and (2) *Everything can be taken from a man but one thing: the last of human freedoms - to choose one's attitude in any given set of circumstances.* Share what you are learning that applies to these quotes. How are you using the space between stimulus and response, and how is that empowering you to choose a more positive attitude?

DIVING DEEPER

Option 1) Practice Being Joyful
GROUP OBSERVATION

Paul uses the Greek word for joy and rejoice 16 times in this little book of Philippians. What does that tell us about a joyful attitude? What stands out to you in the following verses?

Leaders:
Select one or more of the Diving Deeper options to process with your group.

Philippians 3:1 *".... Rejoice in the Lord! It is no trouble for me to write the same thing to you again and it is a safeguard for you."*

Philippians 4:4 *"Rejoice in the Lord always. I will say it again: Rejoice!"*

How do these passages reinforce this concept? What are some additional insights that you find in the following similar verses?

1 Thessalonians 5:16-18 *"Rejoice always, pray continually, give thanks in all circumstances; for this is God's will for you in Christ Jesus."*

James 1:2-4 *"Consider it pure joy, my brothers and sisters, whenever you face trials of many kinds, because you know that the testing of your faith produces perseverance. Let perseverance finish its work so that you may be mature and complete, not lacking anything."*

How does repetition help us get a concept? Are there any other Biblical concepts that seem to be repeated a lot in the Bible?

Life Application: What are some things that you have had to repeatedly practice in order to become good at it? Why would a joyful attitude be something God would want us to become competent in? What are some things that you are trying to change, on the screen of your mind, in order to be more grateful?

Option 2) A Better Obedience
GROUP OBSERVATION

Read the passages below. Who is Paul calling "dogs", and what was so bad about this group to cause Paul to write such a stern warning?

Philippians 3:2-3 *"Watch out for those dogs, those men who do evil, those mutilators of the flesh. For it is we who are the circumcision, we who worship by the Spirit of God, who glory in Christ Jesus, and who put no confidence in the flesh..."*

Philippians 3:2 (MSG) *"Steer clear of the barking dogs, those religious busybodies; all bark and no bite. All they're interested in is appearances—knife-happy circumcisers, I call them."*

In Matthew, Chapter 23, Jesus addresses the teachers of the Law and the Pharisees (potentially a similar group of leaders). Jesus gives seven examples of how they were destroying the true meaning of God's Law. Read the following verses (feel free to examine the whole chapter) and answer, "Why did Jesus also speak out against this group of religious leaders?"

Matthew 23:25-26 *"Woe to you, teachers of the law and Pharisees, you hypocrites! You clean the outside of the cup and dish, but inside they are full of greed and self-indulgence. Blind Pharisee! First clean the inside of the cup and dish, and then the outside also will be clean."*

What does Paul say about his own accomplishments and where they came from in verses 4-6 below? Where does Paul say he found his confidence before coming to Christ and how did that relate to the previously mentioned group of "dogs"?

Philippians 3:4-6 *"If anyone else thinks they have reasons to put confidence in the flesh, I have more:* (**1-Ritual**) *circumcised on the eighth day,* (**2-Race**) *of the people of Israel,* (**3-Religion**) *of the tribe of Benjamin, a Hebrew of Hebrews; in regard to the law, a Pharisee;* (**4-Reputation**) *as for zeal, persecuting the church;* (**5-Rules**) *as for legalistic righteousness, faultless."*

Life Application: Have you ever had a legalist attitude, and if so, what have you noticed about yourself and your perspective of others while being legalistic? Review what Paul said about his "confidence in the flesh" in Philippians 3:4-6 as organized in the categories above (Ritual, Race, Religion, etc.). What might be some contemporary ways we put too much confidence in our flesh? How might you be tempted to put confidence in your flesh?

Option 3) Find Your Ultimate Confidence (Identity) in Christ Jesus
GROUP OBSERVATION

This section might be best called "Paul's profit and loss statement."
Read Philippians 3:7-9 and answer the following questions together as a group:
"But whatever was to my profit I now consider loss for the sake of Christ. What is more, I consider everything a loss compared to the surpassing greatness of knowing Christ Jesus my Lord, for whose sake I have lost all things. I consider them rubbish, that I may gain Christ and be found in him, not having a righteousness of my own that comes from the law, but that which is through faith in Christ--the righteousness that comes from God and is by faith."

• How might these verses give the antidote to the previous issue of legalism?

• Do you think this passage affirms putting one's identity in Christ, if so, how?

Life Application: If you were able to have an identity (a confidence) that came solely from your relationship with Christ, how might that serve as a safeguard for your attitude?

Leaders:
Review the Practice This Week with your group. Either have someone close in prayer or pair-up and pray for each other. Ask God to light something up from this week's material that you will want to focus on to build a better attitude.

PRACTICE THIS WEEK. Choose one or two things you will apply from today's study and report back next week about how you were able to implement the application.

SOAP ASSIGNMENT. Below are the Scriptures to SOAP this next week. If you have never done a SOAP exercise before, review the instructions located in the front of this Study Guide. During your small group time, consider having one or two people share their SOAP with the group, or pair-up and share with one other person.

- **Philippians 3:12-14**
- **2 Corinthians 4:16-18**
- **Philippians 3:20-21**

KIDS & ADULTS

Change the screen. Ask your child, grandchild or mentee what they do when their device (phone, iPad, or TV) has something on the screen that they do not like. Maybe a new show/video or an advertisement pops onto the screen unexpectedly, or a show comes on immediately after they finish one they were watching. How do they react when something they don't like come onto the screen?

The answer is pretty easy, right? They simply change the screen and choose a different show, game or program. Talk with them about how their mind is like the screen of their device. We have things that happen to us all the time that pop into our life or on the screen of our mind and thoughts. Sometimes they are negative experiences, words, thoughts or actions of others.

Rather than get upset, angry or frustrated (you know when we whine about having to take out the trash or pick up the dishes), we can change the screen. We can change what we tell ourselves and quickly make a choice to be patient, kind, ask a question or just choose to have a better attitude - like changing the screen on our device. Explain to them that they are good at changing the screen on their device because they have done it a lot, repeatedly. Illustrate how this can also help them do better at changing the screen of their minds and unwanted thoughts.

Finally, ask them, "If negative stuff is happening to you, are there things you can do, or something you can remind yourself of to keep your outlook positive? Give me some examples."

Leaders:
Use the Kids & Adults section to get feedback on who is using the questions in our material with their kids, grandkids, or mentees? How is that going? What kind of conversations are happening? Celebrate with one another any success stories.

WEEK EIGHT

HOW TO GO THE DISTANCE

THIS WEEK'S THEME.

Spiritual Endurance. In this week's lesson there are five principles from Philippians 3 about how to go the distance -- imitation, examination, elimination, concentration and anticipation. After the attitude check, review each principle and choose one to address personally.

HOW WAS YOUR WEEK?

Take a moment to think about your attitudes this week. Were you more happy or sad or angry? Color in the figure based on the amount of each emotion you felt using the emotions below.

Red--Anger
Blue--Sad
Green--Envy
Yellow--Contentment
Purple--Disgust
Orange--Anxiety
Pink--Grateful

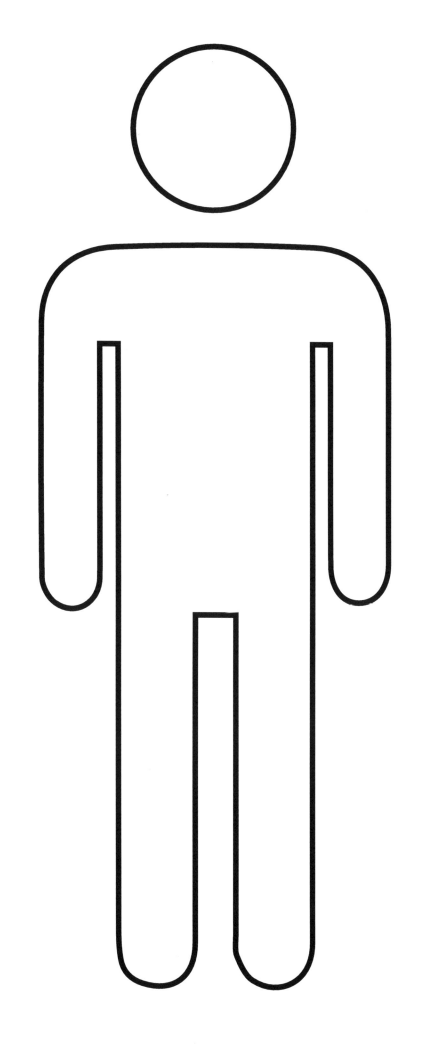

WHAT RACE ARE YOU IN?

Growing up there was no question--no ambiguity to me or anyone who knew me--that I did not like school. I was a terrible student who struggled with an undiagnosed learning disorder that kept me in a place of constant failure and fear of being rejected because of my poor performance. But there was a shining star; a time each year when I loved school and could not wait to arrive and participate in the days activities. It was "Field Day" - the one day when I could truly compete at something I might have a chance to excel at, even win. Why? Because I could run, and I was fast.

I am not that tall. As an adult, 6'1 is no giant. But when you do all your vertical growing in junior high, and you are 6'1, that's pretty tall. The combination of my long legs, and farm feed and breed strength, made me fast. I could never bring home A's, B's or C's, but I could bring home ribbons. And on Field Day, I would bring home a whole collection. I understood what everyone grasps in any kind of race, that when we run, we run to win.

Running is a common metaphor in Scripture for the spiritual journey to which God has called us. That journey, based on the metaphor of running, is one where God wants us to be fully engaged. In Philippians 3:13b-15 (MSG) Paul writes, *"I've got my eye on the goal, where God is beckoning us onward—to Jesus. I'm off and running, and I'm not turning back. So let's keep focused on that goal, those of us who want everything God has for us."*

In 1 Corinthians 9:24 he says, *"Do you not know that in a race all the runners run, but only one gets the prize? Run in such a way as to get the prize."*

For me, in elementary and junior high school, getting the red ribbon prize was what motivated me to do my best. That was my goal! For believers in the spiritual race doing our best is running toward God's goal for us. It's not a subjective goal that we decide on, or one that culture selects for us, but one that God has chosen for us; to be like Christ, to fix our eyes on Jesus, our ultimate model of love, patience, kindness, and compassion.

When we run toward that goal we are forever improving. You see, the truly amazing thing, whether we recognize it or not, is that God has an agenda for what happens to us. Philippians 1:6 told us that He is committed to complete what He has started in us. In verse 2:13, we are reminded that it is *"God who works in you to will and to act according to his good purpose"* And now, Paul challenges us in Philippians 3:12, *"but I press on to take hold of that for which Christ Jesus took hold of me."* The sooner we get on board with God's plan the sooner we'll be bringing home red ribbons.

What did a ribbon mean to me? It was a little piece of the identity that I was craving. I wanted desperately to be seen as someone that mattered—someone who had value and purpose, and was wanted by others. We all want that. We are hardwired to desire connection and community with others that affirms who we are and our place in the world. All of our lives, to one degree or another, we are seeking that identity. If we cannot get it from running a foot race then we'll pursue it from running in the academic race or the race of popularity, talent, charisma, or even rebellion. For some people, what they are really good at is being really bad. Instead of excelling at being good, they excel at being bad.

The real problem where most of us are ignorant, is that whether we're the standout student, the top notch athlete, or the rising renegade, we are all, without Jesus, running the wrong race. If my efforts in life are not creating a better me--one that is more like Christ and aligned with God's goals and intentions for me--it really doesn't matter what I achieve or gain. That's why Paul had such a radical shift in his attitude. That's why he could exclaim, "Whatever was to my profit, I now consider loss for the sake of Christ. What is more, I consider everything a loss compared to the surpassing greatness of knowing Christ Jesus, my Lord."

What race are you in? What are you running for, or from? When we realize that Jesus has called us to run a completely different kind of race, we all of a sudden start finding a different kind of identity. You see, where you find your deepest identity, is where you find your deepest motivation. If my identity is defined by others, I run to please people. If my identity is defined by accomplishments, I run to achieve tasks. If I think I am failing in any of those pursuits, my attitude becomes one of failure, defeat, or hopelessness. But if my identity is defined by Jesus, then I run to be like Him. And when I discover that He is the One that will ultimately see me through, never abandoning me, my attitude (frame of mind) will be filled with the knowledge, confidence and hope, that through it all, with Jesus I'm going to win.

WHAT'S HOLDING YOU BACK?

Philippians 3:12b-15a (MSG) *"I am well on my way, reaching out for Christ, who has so wondrously reached out for me....I've got my eye on the goal, where God is beckoning us onward—to Jesus. I'm off and running, and I'm not turning back. So let's keep focused on that goal, those of us who want everything God has for us."*

Serious runners in a race know the value of planned abandonment. They strip off every weight that could slow them down from reaching their goal. This is also true of believers who understand the same following principle: what hinders us must be thrown off or it will encumber our progress and maybe even sideline us from our spiritual goal.

I have seen many wonderful people, folks I truly care for, get distracted from their spiritual race. It is inevitable. If we fail to identify what needs to be thrown off, we will get pulled off course. I do my level best to sound the alarm and keep the strategy of pursuing Christ as our top goal. Yet, time and again, sweet people get swept away by the cares of this world.

Saddest to me is that it doesn't have to be this way. The vast majority of folks who attend any church are not working a plan and choose instead to simply fly by the seat of their spiritual pants. *"Oh, I know Jesus...yeah, He died for my sin. He's my Savior...I go to church regularly."* Sorry, but that won't cut it! If we are not serious about the spiritual race (running to win) [1Corinthians 9:24], we are going to lose

If we are not serious about the spiritual race, we are going to lose momentum.

momentum, passion, the peace that he wants to give, and the spiritual blessing that He wants us to experience.

We might be saved from hell, but we are not satisfied with heaven. We may have met Jesus, but we are not knowing Him daily. We may have joined a church, but never learned to be the church. We may know who loves us, but no one can tell by our behavior who to love. That is not our calling. You and I can run a good race and finish the course with an amazing sense of satisfaction, pleasure and purpose. If we chart a course, make a plan and follow through, we will see amazing results.

Paul wasn't the only author in Scripture that wanted us to see how our faith is like a race. The author of Hebrews wants us to finish well and to finish strong. In Hebrews 12:1-3, he gives us the fundamental steps to accomplish our calling: 1) throw off everything that hinders, 2) fix our eyes on Jesus, and 3) run with perseverance the race marked out for us.

Learning to throw off what hinders us is no small task because there is a plethora of potential hindrances. Scriptures abound in identifying our spiritual hindrances, but 1 John 2:15-17 puts them into three categories, *"Do not love the world or anything in the world. If anyone loves the world, the love of the Father is not in him. For everything in the world--**the cravings of sinful man, the lust of his eyes and the boasting of what he has and does**--comes not from the Father but from the world. The world and*

its desires pass away, but the man who does the will of God lives forever."

I see three hindrances in the above passage - pleasures, possessions, and pride. God wants us to enjoy creation (1 Timothy 4:4) and what he has given us dominion over (Genesis 2:15). But when the created becomes more important than the Creator, we have just been hindered. We are hindered when pleasing ourselves is more important than pleasing God, when possessions become obsessions, and when we think what we do, or have, makes us more important than others.

Ask yourself, "What is hindering me from living and loving like Jesus?" Stephen Paul says: *"The space for what you want is already filled with what you have settled for instead. Every time you let go of something limiting you create space for something better."*

The first step is **examination**. Letting go of what is limiting us requires more than identification, but we cannot proceed without it. We'll never succeed at changing something that we fail to identify. Max Depree reminds us, "If we always do what we've always done, we'll always be who we've always been." To have the attitude that is best; we first have to identify and own the attitude that we have - the attitude that is holding us back and limiting our ability to reflect Christ and His love.

The second step is **elimination** - planned abandonment. Ask yourself "Does this distraction need to be limited or eliminated?" Some things are fine in moderation, but when they become an obsession, more drastic steps may be needed. What's the plan? If we fail to get specific about when we will actually put limits (or boundaries) around something, or eliminate something that is holding us

back we'll still not move forward.

The final step is **support**. To be successful at this plan and to achieve the desired goal, we will most likely need someone to run with. The four-minute mile, for the longest time was considered impossible. But in 1954, Roger Bannister broke the four minute mark. What is often left out of the story is that he had several pacers - other runners who ran alongside to challenge and inspire him to keep the pace. Without those pace runners, he might not have set the record. The other interesting piece of the story is that within one year of his accomplishment, 14 other runners also broke the four-minute standard. Once someone shows it can be done, others seem to gain momentum in their own achievements.

We need one another! We need to not run alone. We need others to inspire us to keep our pace and to stay the course. So, who are your running partners? Who is seeking Jesus with you, loving others well beside you, and setting a spiritual pace that inspires you to run to win?

HOW TO GO THE DISTANCE

OPEN IN PRAYER. After opening in prayer ask group members to pair up and share with each other what they tried to apply or practice this last week from the previous week's material.

Attitude Check. Review the practice session from last week. Have everyone share their experience. Paul gives an example in this passage about pressing on to win a prize. He seems to be describing a race and being determined to not give up. Ask your group to share any experiences they have had in any kind of long distance or obstacle race. How would a tough mudder or spartan race fit with Paul's analogy for us today?

DIVING DEEPER

Option 1) Imitation: Find Someone To Follow

GROUP OBSERVATION

What do you notice about Paul's encouragement in Philippians 3:17 to follow his example?

Philippians 3:17 *"Join with others in following my example, brothers, and take note of those who live according to the pattern we gave you."*

Life Application: How does Paul's repeated challenge for us to follow his example, by also pointing out good examples and patterns (Timothy and Epaphroditus), inspire you to both, have and be, an example to others?

Leaders:
Select one or more of the Diving Deeper options to process with your group.

Option 2) Examination: Own Up To Your Faults
GROUP OBSERVATION

Read the following Scriptures and take turns answering this question:
Why is "owning up" to past mistakes an important part of endurance?

Philippians 3:12-13a *"Not that I have already obtained all this, or have already been made perfect...I do not consider myself yet to have taken hold of it."*
Lamentations 3:40 *"Let us examine our ways and test them, and let us return to the Lord."*

Proverbs 28:13 (GNT) *"You will never succeed in life if you try to hide your sins. Confess them and give them up; then God will show mercy on you."*

Life Application: How does examination of one's issues and condition contribute to a healthy and humble attitude? Is there anyone in the group that would like to share what they are learning about this principle and how it has impacted their attitude?

Option 3) Elimination: Put the Past Behind You
GROUP OBSERVATION

Reflecting on the following Scriptures, why is putting the past behind us an important skill to be developed?

Philippians 3:13b *"I do not consider myself yet to have taken hold of it. But one thing I do: Forgetting what is behind..."*

Isaiah 43:18-19a *"Forgetting the former things; do not dwell on the past. See, I am doing a new thing! (says the Lord)."*

Luke 9:62 (GNT) *"Jesus said to him, 'Anyone who starts to plow and then keeps looking back is of no use for the Kingdom of God.'"*

Life Application: What parts of our painful past do we need to remember and not forget, and what portion of the past should be forgotten? Can we truly forget what is behind us? What do you think a healthy forgetfulness might look like?

Option 4) Concentration: Focus on the Goal
GROUP OBSERVATION

What do you think is the goal Paul is reaching for? How do the passages on the next page add insight to this question?

Philippians 3:12b-15a (MSG) *"I am well on my way, reaching out for Christ, who has so wondrously reached out for me. ...I've got my eye on the goal, where God is beckoning us onward—to Jesus. I'm off and running, and I'm not turning back. So let's keep focused on that goal, those of us who want everything God has for us."*

Hebrews 12:2a *"Let us fix our eyes on Jesus the author and perfector of our faith."*

2 Corinthians 3:17-18 (NLT) *"For the Lord is the Spirit, and wherever the Spirit of the Lord is, there is freedom. So all of us who have had that veil removed can see and reflect the glory of the Lord. And the Lord—who is the Spirit—makes us more and more like him as we are changed into his glorious image."*

Life Application: What would your life look like if you were fully embracing the goal Paul speaks of, to become more like Jesus?

Option 5) Anticipation: Wait for His Return
GROUP OBSERVATION

What do the following passages tell us about anticipation?

Philippians 3:20-21 *"But our citizenship is in heaven. And we eagerly await a Savior from there, the Lord Jesus Christ, who, by the power that enables him to bring everything under his control, will transform our lowly bodies so that they will be like his glorious body."*

1 Peter 1:13b *"Set your hope fully on the grace to be given you when Jesus Christ is revealed."*

Romans 8:23-25 (NLT) *"And we believers also groan, even though we have the Holy Spirit within us as a foretaste of future glory, for we long for our bodies to be released from sin and suffering. We, too, wait with eager hope for the day when God will give us our full rights as his adopted children, including the new bodies he has promised us. We were given this hope when we were saved. (If we already have something, we don't need to hope for it. But if we look forward to something we don't yet have, we must wait patiently and confidently.)"*

2 Corinthians 4:16-18 *"Therefore we do not lose heart. Though outwardly we are wasting away, yet inwardly we are being renewed day by day. For our light and momentary troubles are achieving for us an eternal glory that far outweighs them all. So we fix our eyes not on what is seen, but on what is unseen, since what is seen is temporary, but what is unseen is eternal."*

Life Application: How does anticipation factor into the believer's life, and what difference (if managed well) could anticipation make in one's attitude or frame of mind?

PRACTICE THIS WEEK. Choose one or two things you will apply from today's study and report back next week about how you were able to implement the application.

SOAP ASSIGNMENT. Below are the Scriptures to SOAP this next week. If you have never done a SOAP exercise before, review the instructions located in the front of this Study Guide. During your small group time, consider having one or two people share their SOAP with the group, or pair-up and share with one other person.
- **Philippians 4:11-13**
- **Psalm 139:23-24**
- **1 Thessalonians 5:16-18**

KIDS & ADULTS

Ask your child, grandchild or mentee if they have seen any of the TV shows about physical endurance: Spartan, American Ninja Warrior, or The Amazing Race? If they have, ask them what they think the competitors (participants) had to do in order to successfully finish the course or get closer to finishing the course? One of the unique things about American Ninja Warrior (ANW) is how many children and youth have been inspired to excel at obstacle competitions because of a favorite ANW competitor.

Together, explore at least one of the following options: (1) The Example Option: Who do you look up to that inspires you to do something better? (If they are struggling to think of someone who does something that inspires them, try to help them think of someone who is an example of having a good attitude); or (2) The Obstacle Option: What are some obstacles we face in life that we might need help with?

Leaders:
Use the Kids & Adults section to get feedback on who is using the questions in our material with their kids, grandkids, or mentees? How is that going? What kind of conversations are happening? Celebrate with one another any success stories.

WEEK NINE

REDUCING STRESS & ANXIETY

THIS WEEK'S THEME.

How to reduce stress and anxiety. Worry and anxiety create unnecessary stress. One can have an anxious attitude. Do you remember what our definition of attitude means? Attitude is one's frame of mind that affects their disposition in life and the relationships around them. Stress and anxiety are the evidence of a certain frame of mind. Worry is just negative or pessimistic meditation.

HOW WAS YOUR WEEK?

Take some time to reflect on the week you had. Think of all the attitudes and emotions you felt. Circle the different attitudes you had this week or list any that aren't here.

HAPPY

WORRY

TRUST

ANGER

ENVY

CONTENT

GRATEFUL

LOVE

ANTICIPATION

PITY

DISGUST

KINDNESS

Have you noticed a difference in your attitude since the start of this study?

_____

_____

_____

_____

_____

_____

_____

_____

_____

_____

_____

_____

_____

CHOOSE YOUR PROBLEMS

Everyone has stress, but not everyone has to be controlled by their stress. The choice is yours. I have always been a fan of the little statement: "We can pick our problems." Problems are inevitable, but what problems you have are yours to choose.

OK, if you are anything like me, that statement isn't one that you easily agree with. Something in us pushes back and says, that's not true. I remember one time saying something similar in a sermon that was so dissonant to a person in the audience, he couldn't contain himself. He just blurted out, loud enough for everyone to hear, "That's not true!" Wherever you are, if you want to blurt out and yell, "That's not true!" - be my guest. Maybe it'll make you feel a little better.

But, before you go shouting all over the place that Pastor Jeff is saying stuff that just isn't true, hear me out. Maybe it is true. Maybe you have more power than you know. Maybe you not only have problems, but perhaps you are choosing the wrong problems, and today you can begin to choose better one's.

Problem free? I don't think so. Sure, I guess if we were really, really powerful we could choose to just not have problems. But even Jesus couldn't, or at least didn't, make that choice. In John 16:33, Jesus said something pretty disheartening (at least at first), *"In this world you will have trouble."* There you go. God Himself is basically saying - as long as you are here, you are going to have problems (troubles). Then He continues by giving us hope, *"But take heart! I have overcome the world."*

You see, if Jesus has overcome the world, and He is in me and I am in Him, then I too can overcome the world. I don't have to be overcome by the troubles of this world, I can overcome them.

So, how do we go about picking better problems, and overcoming them? Let's think about it. If you choose to steal something, you have just chosen a whole set of problems. You have chosen a level of inner discord because you know that you should not take what isn't yours. You just chose to be in violation with the law and could therefore have issues with those who enforce the law. When you are arrested for stealing, you are experiencing the problems that came with that choice.

If you choose to have an affair, you are choosing a collection of problems that are built right into that choice. Guilt, shame, deception, regret, conflict, maybe divorce, separation or even murder. Yikes! I'm not saying you will get all of those, but the further you go down a path of toxic choices, the deeper and more toxic those problems are.

On the other hand, if I choose not to talk through a conflict with my spouse when I haven't followed through on some task that I promised to do, that is the problem I've chosen. If I choose to be defensive and blame her for some aspect of my irresponsibility, I'll get a different set of problems. If I seek to avoid the conversation altogether, that choice will produce yet another set of problems. Are you tracking with me?

If we give our child a consequence for something he didn't do, and he's pouty and grumpy, that's the problem we choose. If my wife and I stick together and work out our differences, that's the problem we choose. For the person who is in the middle of their third divorce, because they don't want to work it out, that's the problem they choose. We pick our problems.

How you decide to react to, talk out, avoid, procrastinate, run away from or fight through your problems, are all choices that you are making. No matter what your problems are they are going to either get better or worse, depending on what you choose to do with them.

If I have cancer, I didn't choose that, but I can choose what I do with my cancer. If I am cheated on by someone, I didn't choose that, but whether I get violent, silent or lovingly confront that issue is my choice. And the choice I make will either escalate or de-escalate the problem - I choose.

Attitude is always a choice. When you choose a bad attitude, then you will inherit some additional problems that will follow that choice. When you choose to have a good attitude, there are some additional shifts that will follow that choice. We will always have troubles, problems, and difficulties in life, but the level in which you struggle, and the amount of your struggle (the increase or the decrease) is up to you.

In Philippians 4:4, Paul gives us some great advice about how to pick really good problems. He says, *"Rejoice in the Lord always. I will say it again, rejoice."* The more we cultivate a frame of mind that believes God is at work, and is always working to bring good from evil, the more we will be able to choose and maintain an attitude of gratitude regardless of the problems and troubles we experience in this life.

It's our choice. We can choose to rejoice or to grumble. We can choose to see the good that God is doing (believing He's always at work to do good), or decide to believe otherwise - that He's not doing anything good and for some reason isn't going to. What we tell ourselves about God in the midst of our problem will determine which problems we choose. And, whichever one we choose, will have repercussions.

The Scriptures are very clear. When we choose to walk in obedience, we get a certain kind of problem. And when we choose to be disobedient, we get another kind of problem. The sooner we figure out what kind of problems we want, the better off we'll be. So, what kind of problems are you choosing?

SOW A THOUGHT

Philippians 4:4-7 *"Rejoice in the Lord always. I will say it again: Rejoice! Let your gentleness be evident to all. The Lord is near. Do not be anxious about anything, but in everything, by prayer and petition, with thanksgiving, present your requests to God. And the peace of God, which transcends all understanding, will guard your hearts and your minds in Christ Jesus."*

> Sow a thought, reap and attitude;
> sow an attitude, reap an action;
> sow an action, reap a habit;
> sow a habit, reap a character;
> sow a character, reap a destiny.

The way in which we think, will determine the way in which we will go. Proverbs 23:7 (KJV) says, *"As he thinketh in his heart, so is he."* James Allen says, in his classic book, *As a Man Thinketh, "A man's mind may be likened unto a garden which can be intelligently cultivated or allowed to run wild. But, whether cultivated or neglected, it must and will bring forth, each to its own kind. If no useful seeds are put into it than an abundance of useless weed seed will fall therein and continue to produce their kind."*

Reducing our stress is directly connected to the law of the sower. Galatians 6:7b-8 says, *"A man reaps what he sows. The one who sows to please his sinful nature, from that nature will reap destruction; the one who sows to please the spirit, from the spirit will reap eternal life."*

In the fourth chapter of Philippians, Paul gives us some simple instruction about how to reduce our stress and live out the peace that Christ offers us. When I allow negative thought patterns to fill my mind, I will reap negatives repercussions. Rejoicing always (Philippians 4:4) isn't just some spiritual platitude; it is one of the keys to a higher, more positive spiritual attitude. When people who profess to be believers are filled with negativity, dissension, criticism, and pessimism they are sabotaging, in their own life and sometimes those around them, what God can and wants to do. They literally disconnect themselves from God's agenda.

Conversely, when we sow or focus our thoughts on what God has promised and engage him authentically and thankfully, we are not only exercising our faith and making it stronger, but we are also building our confidence in Jesus and what he promised to do when we turn our worries into prayers.

Prayer is, and always has been, an invitation into authentic relationship with God. The God who is forever with us, wants nothing more than to be enlarged within us. That only happens out of true and authentic interaction. Jesus said in John 4:23-24 (MSG) *"It's who you are and the way you live that count before God. Your worship must engage your spirit in the pursuit of truth. That's the kind of people the Father is out looking for: those who are simply and honestly themselves before him in their worship."* The greater our authentic connection and submission to truth, the greater the effect it will have on our attitude and ability to spiritually step into the "peace the transcends all understanding".

I can authentically complain or speak about my anxiety or worry to God, but if I fail to *cast my cares upon him* (1 Peter 5:7), I am only talking at God, not interacting with Him. The idea of casting one's cares is shifting the weight from me to Him. When I say that I've prayed and given my worries to God, but continue to try and sort them out in my own strength nothing has shifted - the weight, load, pressure and stress is still on me.

When I practice prayer at a relational level I am not only talking, I am listening. I begin to hear the Spirit tell me to rejoice because He's got me covered. It is in the relationship with God that His Spirit joins with our spirit to affirm that we are His children (Rom 8:15-16). This is when my attitude shifts to one of serenity instead of stress, trust instead of fear, and to faith instead of doubt.

When I remind myself, that what God says is true, and then act upon that message, it becomes a new habit, a new practice. It is this practice of telling myself the truth and then acting on that truth, that gradually changes my character; who I am. That in turn, builds my confidence in God and the destiny He has promised me. Those who are learning to master their attitude are at the deepest level simply trusting their Master. They've learned how to take their own words (thought messages) captive and take God at His word.

REDUCING STRESS & ANXIETY

OPEN IN PRAYER. After opening in prayer ask group members to pair up and share with each other what they have tried to apply or practice this last week from the previous weeks' material.

Attitude Check. Review the practice session from last week. Have everyone share their experience. Let's face this together. We all have anxiety at some level but we don't need to let that anxiety grow. Instead we can develop the skills that reduce our stress and anxiety. Remind the group of some of my (Pastor Jeff's) symptoms: (1) Physical symptoms--the twitching of my eye and bouncing of my foot or leg; and (2) Emotional symptoms--fear of rejection or failure.

As a group, share some of your symptoms of anxiety. How are you learning to recognize when anxiety is lurking? Have someone close with a short prayer asking God to give us more freedom; to be honest about our anxiety and then to reduce and conquer it.

DIVING DEEPER

Option 1) Worry About Nothing
GROUP OBSERVATION

What are some of the insights that these scriptures give about worry and anxiety?

Philippians 4:6a *"Do not be anxious about anything."*

Matthew 6:34 (Jesus) *"Therefore, do not worry about tomorrow, for tomorrow will worry about itself. Each day has enough troubles of its own."*

Psalm 139:23-24 *"Search me, O God, and know my heart; test me and know my anxious thoughts. See if there is any offensive way in me, and lead me in the way everlasting."*

Life Application: I say often that I have come to appreciate anxiety. It is like a light on my spiritual dashboard that alerts me to something I am trying to control versus trusting God. What are some signs that you are anxious and how does anxiety affect your attitude?

Option 2) Pray About Everything
GROUP OBSERVATION

Read the following verses together. What does Paul say we should do instead of worry?

Philippians 4:6b *"But in everything, by prayer and petition, with thanksgiving present your requests to God."*

Romans 12:12 *"Be...patient in affliction, faithful in prayer."*

1 Thessalonians 5:17-18 *"Pray continually, give thanks in all circumstances, for this is God's will for you in Christ Jesus."*

Life Application: The passages above seem to be suggesting that prayer (communication with God) is pervasive. How do you think someone can synthesize prayer into all of life?

Option 3) Thank God In Everything
GROUP OBSERVATION

Thanking God in everything is no small concept in Scripture. It could seem an impossible task. What do you think these passages are telling us?

Philippians 4:6b *"But in everything...with thanksgiving..."*

1 Thessalonians 5:16-18 *"Be joyful always, pray continually, give thanks in all circumstances, for this is God's will for you in Christ Jesus."*

Romans 12:12 *"Be joyful in hope, patient in affliction, faithful in prayer."*

Ephesians 5:20 *"Always giving thanks to God the Father for everything, in the name of our Lord Jesus Christ."*

Life Application: One of our core disciplines or habits, (that I speak of often) is the habit of gratitude. How does the cultivation of this discipline make the commands in these Scriptures more attainable? How can we cultivate this more in our marriages, families and church?

Option 4) Think About The Right Things
GROUP OBSERVATION

How does Philippians 4:8 tie into the concept of attitude and the definition that we have been using in our series?

Attitude Definition: one's frame of mind that affects their disposition in life and the relationships around them.

Philippians 4:8 (NIV) *"Finally, brothers and sisters, whatever is true, whatever is noble, whatever is right, whatever is pure, whatever is lovely, whatever is admirable—if anything is excellent or praiseworthy—think about such things."*

Life Application: Have you been doing anything different in the management of your thoughts since the start of our Attitude series? If so, what? If not, what do you think has held you back?

PRACTICE THIS WEEK. Choose one or two things you will apply from today's study and report back next week about how you were able to implement the application.

Leaders:
Review the Practice This Week with your group. Ask someone in your group to close your time in prayer.

SOAP ASSIGNMENT. Below are the Scriptures to SOAP this next week. If you have never done a SOAP exercise before, review the instructions located in the front of this Study Guide. During your small group time, consider having one or two people share their SOAP with the group, or pair-up and share with one other person.
- Philippians 4:10-13
- 2 Corinthians 12:9-10
- Matthew 6:31-33

KIDS & ADULTS

If we all have anxiety, it is huge to realize that it starts, for the most part, when we are kids. One of the most powerful ways to begin dealing with our anxiety is to be aware that it is happening and learn how to confront the thought that accompanies the anxiety.

Read the following scripture with your youth. Then have them draw a picture of what they think it feels like to be worried.

Philippians 4:6-7 *"Don't worry about anything. No matter what happens, tell God about everything. Ask and pray, and give thanks to him. Then God's peace will watch over your hearts and your minds. He will do this because you belong to Christ Jesus. God's peace can never be completely understood."*

Ask them to explain their picture to you. Then ask if there was ever a time they felt afraid or worried, like in the picture. You can use Scriptures like Psalm 91:3-4 or Isaiah 41:10 to reassure them that God will help them with their fear or anxiety, and that sometimes their thoughts can cause fears or worries that aren't real or true.

Help them memorize Philippians 4:6-7, Isaiah 41:10 and/or 2 Timothy 1:7. Explain that they can pray and read these scriptures out loud whenever they feel afraid or anxious about anything, and God will bring them peace.

Leaders:
Use the Kids & Adults section to get feedback on who is using the questions in our material with their kids, grandkids, or mentees? How is that going? What kind of conversations are happening? Celebrate with one another any success stories.

WEEK TEN

LEARNING THE SECRET TO SATISFACTION

THIS WEEK'S THEME.

Spiritual Contentment. Contentment is one of the most critical skills to learn in order to master one's attitude. We will see four practical ways to learn how to be content regardless of what our circumstances tell us.

HOW WAS YOUR WEEK?

Remember those car games you'd play as a kid on a roadtrip? Let's do one with your small group. One person starts followed by the rest of the group saying part of a sentence. Leave your sentence hanging for the next person to finish in an interesting way. The crazier the better!

Example:

Person 1: One day I went to the...

Person 2: ...store and was met by...

Person 3: ...a giant talking bear.

THE THIEF OF JOY

When the Bible speaks of and calls us to contentment, it's not challenging us to be apathetic about changing what is in our power to change, but to not let what we cannot change steal our joy. It isn't about settling for whatever happens, but rather not losing our joy despite what does happen. And furthermore, it's not about caring less about our circumstances, but not allowing our circumstances to diminish how much we care.

Biblical contentment is the supernatural ability and learned skill of finding our joy and happiness in Christ rather than any other thing. That is the *attitude* of Christ - realizing that the power of His presence is experienced when we can actualize true and ultimate meaning and purpose in Him. It comes to life each time we step into His will instead of trying to push through our will. It is the great release of our control and the great embrace of trusting in His control.

Think with me about what we have seen in the Book of Philippians. Take notice of the following statements that are rooted and attached to the relational stability and mental frame of mind that rise out of knowing Jesus:

• *"**Being confident** in this, that **he** who began a good work in you will carry it on to completion . . ."* (Philippians 1:6). Notice the confidence that comes out of his relationship with Christ.

• Concerning those preaching Christ out of *"envy and rivalry"* Paul says, *"**Whether from false motives or true,** Christ is preached. And because of this I rejoice."* (Philippians 1:18b). Notice his confidence that God will work even when others' motives are impure.

• *"**Whatever** happens, conduct yourselves in a manner worthy of the **gospel of Christ**."* (Philippians 1:27a). Notice the behavioral shift (how we choose to conduct ourselves) that comes from the good news of Jesus.

• *"Do nothing out of selfish ambition or vain conceit, but **in humility consider** others better than yourselves."* Notice how changing our frame of mind (to consider others) is exactly what Jesus did, *"(He) did not **consider** equality with God something to be grasped."* (Philippians 2:3, 6). **He humbles** himself.

• *"I consider everything a loss compared to the **surpassing greatness of knowing** Christ Jesus my Lord."* (Philippians 3:8a). Notice how his perspective changed about everything because of knowing Jesus.

• *"We eagerly await a Savior from there, the Lord Jesus Christ, who, by the power that enables him to bring everything under **his control, will transform** our lowly bodies to be like his glorious body."* (Philippians 3:20b-21). Notice Paul's focus and trust in Christ's control and our ultimate transformation through him.

• *"Do not be **anxious** about anything, but in everything **by prayer and petition, with thanksgiving,** present your requests to God and the **peace of God** which transcends all understanding, will guard your hearts and minds in Christ Jesus."* (Philippians 4:6-7). Notice the mental shift from anxiety to peace through prayerful engagement.

• *"I am not saying this because I am in need, for I have learned to be content whatever the circumstances...I can do all of this through him who gives me strength."* (Philippians 4:11, 13). <u>Notice</u> how Jesus changes everything when we let him teach us and equip us to change our mind.

Comparison steals my joy because it alters my frame of mind and takes my focus off of Jesus, and puts it on someone or something else. Instead of being empowered by what I have in my relationship with Christ, I am distracted by what I don't have, giving that thought power over my attitude.

In each of the passages above Paul could have allowed comparison to steal his joy but instead he defeated the thief with the confidence he possessed from his relationship with Jesus. Our attitude changes when our relationship with Jesus changes enough for Him to be where we run with our thoughts.

LOCUS OF CONTROL

"Happiness does not come from a certain set of circumstances but rather a certain set of attitudes."
-Hugh Downs

Becoming someone who has learned to live above their circumstances rather than being consumed by their circumstances is what our Attitude study has been all about. Philippians 4:11 describes that person as being content in any and every circumstance. Someone who finds joy and can maintain their joy apart from the conditions around them, have not an external, but internal locus of control.

The concept behind a ***locus of control***, is a person's belief about what they can or cannot control. The word "locus" comes from the Latin meaning "place" - where we are either *affected* by our circumstances or *affect* our circumstances. If I believe what I am doing on the inside changes how I experience life on the outside, then I have an internal locus of control. If I believe I am helpless and primarily impacted or affected by the things outside of me, I have an external locus of control. So, if I believe others or circumstances are to blame for my attitude, my locus of control is external. Your choice becomes your perception of reality.

How thick is your head? Your head (that thing on the top of your shoulders) is by and large, the same thickness as anyone else's. Yet we often describe others (seldom this is our issue - or is it?) as being *thick-headed*. Of course we know that we are not talking about the literal metrics of the skull, but rather the figurative distance between an issue being communicated, and our acceptance or comprehension of the fact or concept in question. We'll say, "he just can't get it through his *thick head*

that he's in trouble", or "loved," or "has a problem," or "needs to ask for help," etc.

We also have other similar idioms that we use:
- Don't stick your *head in the sand*;
- Don't be so *hard-headed*;
- She's so *bull-headed*;
- You're as *stubborn as on ox*;
- *Catch a clue*;
- Pull your *head out*;
- The lights are on, but nobody's home; and
- He's a few bricks short of a full load.

All of these are about how slow we, as people, can be to take ownership of some truth that is alluding us. Becoming someone who has learned to experience life as an adventure, a gift from God to be enjoyed, and an opportunity to embrace God's blessings, is far from normal. That's the point! God hasn't called us to be normal (of this world) limited to flesh and bones. He's called us into a new dimension of reality. The Biblical authors understood this at the core of who they were, because their core (their internal awareness and being) had changed. What drove them, inspired them and motivated them, had been altered by the indwelling Messiah, the Christ, the One who came to save us and then inhabit us with His presence.

Yeah...I get how that might sound over the top, but it's true! And until we embrace that truth we'll never experience the freedom that Jesus offers and promised to those who know him, love him and are called according to His purposes (Jeremiah 29:11; Romans 8:28; 1 Corinthians 1:21). We will be held captive by lies until we learn to embrace, at a deeper level, the truth that can set us free.

The Bible doesn't use the above idioms to describe the hardness or thickness of our heads. But it does use similar idioms to describe our hearts (our core/internal condition). Consider these scriptures: *"They made their hearts as hard as flint..."* (Zechariah 7:12); *"..because of your stubbornness and unrepentant heart..."* (Romans 2:5); (Jesus) *"because your hearts were hard..."* (Mark 10:5); *"[He who] closes his heart..."* (1 John 3:17, NASB); and *"Today, if you hear his voice, do not harden your hearts..."* (Hebrews 3:7-8).

The heart represents the core of what drives us. It's our internal/motivational center. Therefore, we hear the Scripture guiding us to: *"guard your heart..."* (Proverbs 4:23); *"Create in me a pure heart."* (Psalm 51:10); *"God is the strength of my heart..."* (Psalm 73:26); *"Blessed are the pure in heart..."* (Matthew 5:8); *"Love the Lord your God with all your heart..."* (Luke 10:27); and *"A good man brings good things out of the good stored up in His heart...For out of the overflow of his heart the mouth speaks"* (Luke 6:45).

Attitude, at its core, is an internal/heart issue. The mind and the heart are so closely related that they catch one another's diseases. Think of your heart as the core of your being. Engaging the heart is an act of the will; it is a decision that has to be made over and over until it becomes second nature. It has to become our new normal. This is the fundamental skill that we have been seeking to cultivate.

The more we refine this spiritual discipline, the more we will enjoy the fruit of His presence. When we make the fellowship of His Spirit--engaging His Spirit within us and dialoguing with Him--the more God's word becomes the meditation of our thoughts; the more we cast our anxiety on Him; the more we will see the transformation of our heart, soul, and mind. As we cultivate this internal locus of control (the Spirit and mind of Christ), we will experience an attitude of gratitude, an openness to others, an ability to rise above the circumstances around us and learn to be content in any and every circumstance.

When this is becoming our new normal, we are learning that we are not defined by the external circumstances around us, but by the One who lives within us. Practicing His presence, taking our thoughts captive, adjusting our frame of mind, are all interrelated spiritual skills that align us to Christ's internal presence. As we learn to live out the in-living presence of Jesus, our attitude begins to consistently conform to His likeness.

Lord, continue to soften our hearts and our heads, let us not be closed-minded but always open to you and the work you want to accomplish in us and through us. Use our attitude as a light in this dark world. Greater is He who is in us than he who is in the world!

LEARNING THE SECRET TO SATISFACTION

OPEN IN PRAYER. After opening in prayer ask group members to pair up and share with each other what they tried to apply or practice this last week from the previous weeks material?

Attitude Check. As a group, define the word contentment. Discuss how it can be both a good and a bad thing. How can either perspective affect one's attitude? This week we will be addressing how contentment, from a Biblical perspective, is not just a good thing but a crucial thing for maintaining an ongoing Christ-like attitude. That being said, there is a valid perspective that if we fail to have passion for good things (growth and spiritual health) because we are "content" to be lazy, unfriendly, or unproductive, that our so called "contentment" becomes something that inhibits the character and attitude of Christ.

DIVING DEEPER

Option 1) Avoid Comparison

GROUP OBSERVATION

How does the habit of comparison exacerbate an attitude of greed and discontentment?

2 Corinthians 10:12 *"We do not dare to classify or compare ourselves ...When they measure themselves by themselves and compare themselves with themselves, they are not wise."*

Misconceptions about happiness;
· I must have what others have to be happy.
· I must be liked by everyone to be happy.
· I must acquire more stuff to be happy.

Life Application: What are some things you can tell yourself that would move your thoughts away from unhealthy comparison? (Remember that our attitude is a reflection of what we are telling ourselves - our frame of mind).

Romans 12:15 *"Rejoice with those who rejoice. Mourn with those who mourn."*

Option 2) Adjust to Change
GROUP OBSERVATION

How does Paul's juxtaposition of the following Scriptures illustrate our need for being equipped to adjust to change?

Philippians 4:11b-12a *"I have learned to be content whatever the circumstances. I know what it is to be...*
- **in need**   and I know what it is to **have plenty**."

Philippians 4:12b *"I have learned the secret of being content in any and every situation, whether...*
- **well fed**   or **hungry**,
- **living in plenty**   or **in want**."

Life Application: We often use the idiom "roll with the punches" to describe someone who is able to adjust to change. What do we need, to be a person who can "roll with the punches"?

Option 3) Access Christ's Power
GROUP OBSERVATION

Read the following verses. In the context of these two passages what is Paul saying he is able to do because of the strength or power Christ is giving him? Notice the difference in verse 13 of the newest NIV (2011) and the earlier version below it. What has been changed and why do you think this change was made?

Leaders:
Sometimes the passage "we can do all things" is misquoted to mean that we can do "anything" through Christ as if He were a magic power. Help your group to understand the truth—that Christ enables us to be content through difficulties in life, not to accomplish some impossible task.

Philippians 4:11b-13 (NIV 2011) *"I have learned to be content whatever the circumstances. I know what it is to be in need, and I know what it is to have plenty. I have learned the secret of being content in any and every situation, whether well fed or hungry, whether living in plenty or in want. I can do all this through him who gives me strength."*

Philippians 4:13 *"I can do everything through him who gives me strength."*

2 Corinthians 12:9-10 *"But he said to me, "My grace is sufficient for you, for my power is made perfect in weakness." Therefore I will boast all the more gladly about my weaknesses, so that Christ's power may rest on me. That is why, for Christ's sake, I delight in weaknesses, in insults, in hardships, in persecutions, in difficulties. For when I am weak, then I am strong."*

Life Application: How does Jesus' grace empower us to deal with difficulty and hardship and what is needed to access this power from God?

Option 4) Accept God's Provision
GROUP OBSERVATION

Leaders:
Since this is the last week in our Attitude series, have your group share some of the ways they are learning to have a healthier (more Christ-like) attitude by processing the following questions together: Are you less reactive? How is the space in between stimulus and response changing for you? How have your discussions with the youth in your life been impacted by the Kids & Adults conversations? What are the new skills or practices that are helping you the most?

What does this passage from Paul and the Matthew passage from Jesus tell us that God is promising to do and what should our response be to this promise?

Philippians 4:19 (NIV) *"And my God will meet all your needs according to the riches of his glory in Christ Jesus."*

Matthew 6:31-33 (MSG) *"What I'm trying to do here is to get you to relax, to not be so preoccupied with getting, so you can respond to God's giving. People who don't know God and the way he works fuss over these things, but you know both God and how he works. Steep your life in God-reality, God-initiative, God-provisions. Don't worry about missing out. You'll find all your everyday human concerns will be met."*

Life Application: How is trust a frame of mind, and what are some ways you have learned to trust God more and adjust your frame of mind positively throughout our series?

Attitude Definition: one's frame of mind that affects their disposition in life and the relationships around them.

PRACTICE THIS WEEK. Choose one or two things you will apply from today's study and email or text your group about how you were able to implement the application.

CLOSING YOUR TIME. As a group you have been prompted along the way to be thinking about what's next? Doing life with others is such a powerful way to grow and develop as believers. Before you finish your material, decide and agree upon what your group will do next. Will you take a short break or go right into more material? What material will you do?

Please fill out the online evaluation of our Attitude study and let us know your thoughts. Thank you for being part of this journey of learning how to change our frame of mind and adjust our attitudes to better reflect Christ in the face of life's challenges. We hope that you have grown in your love for, and walk with, Jesus and our church family.

 **KIDS & ADULTS** Choose between one of the following two conversations to discuss with your child/grandchild or mentee.

Option 1 - Do you think happiness is more about what we have (possess) or who we are? Is happiness more about what is going on inside of us, or outside of us? See if they can articulate how we have the ability to choose our attitude (what we tell ourselves) from the inside about a circumstance versus needing all of our circumstances to go well. Together, brainstorm some examples of unfortunate circumstances that can happen, and how we can still choose a positive response.

Option 2 - Have you ever noticed that we (as people) have a tendency to compare ourselves with other? Tease this out a little more by explaining that this isn't a good thing to do, and yet we all do it. It's a habit. Because of our sin nature, bad habits come easily, but good habits have to be worked on. Ask them if there are some things that we are more inclined to compare such as, possessions, looks or friendships? See if they can articulate some examples.

Leaders:
Use the Kids & Adults section to get feedback on who is using the questions in our material with their kids, grandkids, or mentees? How is that going? What kind of conversations are happening? Celebrate with one another any success stories.

APPENDIX

APPENDIX 1
LEADERS:
GETTING STARTED

Your First Group Meeting

1. If your group is meeting for the first time or if new people have joined your group, take time right now to introduce yourselves to each other.

2. Open in prayer and then start your meeting with an icebreaker question that is easy for anyone to answer. This will get the conversation flowing and help the group members transition from their busy days into the group discussion. You may want to consider starting with icebreaker questions each week before diving into the material.

3. Read the YC Group Guidelines and have members review and sign the Grow Group Guidelines (See Appendix 3/Page 152). This will help set the tone for your group meetings and prevent having to address potentially destructive group dynamics as they arise.

4. Watch the 5-10 minute video clip by Pastor Jeff. Then proceed with the Study Guide Discussion format for Week 1.

Gathering a Group

As you are starting your new group or adding to an existing group, the best place to start is to think about the people in your life who would enjoy a study like this. Some of those people may attend your church, but don't stop there. Think about all of your relationships: friends, neighbors, co-workers, relatives and others. In fact, make a list of these folks and pray about inviting them to your group.

If you're stuck, then look at your cell phone. Who are the last 20 people you have called? Okay, you're probably not going to invite your dentist or your children's teachers, but you might. Your frequently called (or texted) numbers reveal the people you are in regular contact with. Put them on your prayer list too.

Then, pray. Pray about inviting the people who are on your list. And, pray about people who are not on your list. Ask God who He would like for you to invite to your group, then pay attention to who crosses your path in the next few days. If you ask, God will bring people to your group.

But, don't stop with just your list. If you have a co-leader, ask him or her to create a list. As you invite people to your group, ask them who they would like to invite to the group. Before you know it, you will have a room full of people ready to join you in the study.

APPENDIX 2
FREQUENTLY
ASKED QUESTIONS

1. How long should we plan for the meeting?

You should plan for a 90 minute to 2 hour meeting to allow for sufficient time for socializing, discussion, and prayer. Start your meeting on time, even if a few people are running late. By starting on time, the late group members will be apologetic and will figure out that the group is serious about starting on time. If you wait for them, then you are reinforcing their lateness. They will learn that the group will wait for them, so they don't need to show up until 15 minutes after the stated start time.

You also want to end the meeting on time. If your group meets on a "school night," then parents will be anxious to get the children home and to bed — not to mention they need to go to work in the morning. After the discussion and prayer time, let people know that if they need to go, then they are welcome to do so. But if they'd like to stay, then they can do that also. This doesn't make it awkward for people if they need to get going.

2. What if we don't cover all of the questions?

The goal of the group meeting is not to cover all of the questions, but to use the questions as a tool for facilitating the group discussion. As the group leader, take time before the meeting to decide which sections will be core to your group discussion. If you have time to get to the rest of the questions, feel free to do so, but don't feel obligated to ask and answer every question in the lesson.

3. Should the leader ever interrupt a group member who is sharing something?

This is a tricky one that depends on what is being shared and why. If it's clear that the person is going down a rabbit trail, then you should redirect them when they take a breath. Say something like, "That's a very interesting thought, but we're going to have to save that discussion for another time" or "I'm really interested in what you're saying, maybe we can continue that conversation after the meeting."

Be sensitive. If the group member is sharing something personal, you might want to give them some space to talk about what's on their heart. If this turns into a pattern every week, then you should redirect the discussion. If you're unsure about what to do, reach out to your coach or your small group pastor. Before you cut them off, say a quick prayer and ask for the Holy Spirit's guidance in how to handle the situation.

4. Is it okay to serve alcoholic beverages in the group?

Serving alcoholic beverages is not a good idea in small group meetings. Since the church is a place where broken people come for healing, some of that brokenness centers around substance abuse. In the case of the small group, it's best to practice what the Bible says in 1 Corinthians 8 and abstain for the sake of others.

5. How should the room be arranged?

The furniture should be arranged so everyone in the group can see each other. Couches can be a challenge, in that, if three people are sitting on the couch, then the people on either end can't see each other. It's better to add more chairs than to create blind spots in the meeting room.

Also, groups do better meeting indoors rather than outdoors. Unless the group meeting is in a very remote location, meeting outdoors often stifles the discussion because group members are afraid of being overheard by the neighbors.

6. What happens if the group is too big for the room?

If your group is larger than eight people, you should subgroup for the discussion. This will not only make the seating arrangement more comfortable, but it will also allow everyone to get a word in. The group can crowd in to watch the video together, then break up into smaller groups for the discussion. You might even break into yet smaller groups of three or four people for the prayer time.

APPENDIX 3
GROW GROUP
AGREEMENT

Leader _____   Apprentice _____

1. We will grow as loving disciples through the following study/ material:
_____

2. We will meet for _____ weeks, after which we will evaluate our direction.

3. We will gather from _____ to _____, each _____ day(s) and make every effort
   to arrive on time so we can start and end on time.

4. We will gather at _____(place)

5. We will Connect daily with God by practicing the following:
   (As a group review the disciplines then ask the grow group members to select 1 or
   more they will work on personally for the duration of your study)

Bible Reading	Meditation	Memorization
Study	Worship	Prayer
Gratitude	Fasting	Petition
Solitude/Silence	Examination & Elimination	Sabbath

6. We will Grow with community by practicing the following:
   (As a group review the Grow disciplines and select 1 or more to practice together each time you meet.)

Accountability	Fellowship	Sharing Resources
Memorization	Hospitality	Encouragement
Cooperation	Gratitude	Intercession
Confession	Worship	

7. We will Serve with love by doing the following:
   (Review the service options then select one to do together as a group. And encourage members to select one to work on individually)

Mentoring/ Discipleship	Community Impact Team (Love INC)	Evangelism
Stewardship/ Financial Giving	Planned Service/ Ministry Team	Spontaneous Service

8. We will agree to the group guidelines.

9. We will seek to share some or all of the following roles and responsibilities (if applicable): leader, apprentice, subgroup leader, host, prayer coordinator, event planner, administrator, service project coordinator, etc.

10. We will confidentially maintain our community through group text messages, email or the use of social media (i.e. Facebook, Twitter etc.), as appropriate.

APPENDIX 4
GROW GROUP
GUIDELINES

Be prepared
If your group is doing the material or reading a book, be prepared by doing your material well before the group meets. Avoid procrastination. Doing your homework early without being rushed will benefit you and the group.

Stay on topic
Getting off topic is sometimes call a "rabbit trail". This will happen, just redirect your group back to the intended conversation. You might say, "ok, we got off track a little, let's go back to our question/topic."

Limit your sharing
Recognize that time is limited. Be considerate of others' desire and need to share.

Use "I" statements
"I" statements are a great way to take ownership and responsibility. For example, "I feel defensive" versus "you always attack me."

Learn to really listen
Being a good listener is more than not talking. Listen for what is being said, reflect what is being said and listen for the emotion underneath what is being said.

Don't fix
Unsolicited advice is taken as criticism. Empower each person to ask for input or direction, if they desire it. If you feel like you have a clear piece of wisdom that would be beneficial, as permission to share. For example, "are you open to hearing another perspective?"

Don't rescue
Try to avoid jumping in too soon to give an answer or move directly to prayer. Let them have a little space to "think out loud" about their struggles or ideas. Ask a question instead of giving an answer. For example, "how would you like to handle that situation? How does that make you feel?"

We don't all have to agree
It is OK to disagree. We don't have to all see everything the same. This shows a great deal of respect for one another. Try whenever possible to let the Word of God be the guide, such as, "what does the Bible say about this topic?"

Be transparent - no side conversation
Anytime we engage in a side conversation, it sends a message that we are not listening.

Confidentiality
In order for people to build trust they must know that what is shared in group stays in group. This does not mean the vacation trip to Disneyland that a group member took, but the things that are private and personal should be kept in confidence unless you have permission to share it outside the group.

Signature_____Date_____

APPENDIX

APPENDIX 5
GROW GROUP
ROSTER

Name	Email	Cell Phone

156